Golden Wisdom for Today's Woman

Treasured Portraits of Faith

By Barbara Sims

Life Journey™ is an imprint of
Cook Communications Ministries, Colorado Springs, Colorado 80918
Cook Communications, Paris, Ontario
Kingsway Communications, Eastbourne, England

GOLDEN WISDOM FOR TODAY'S WOMAN

Printed in the United States of America.

1 2 3 4 5 6 7 8 9 10 Printing/Year 07 06 05 04 03

Unless otherwise noted, all Scripture references are from the Holy Bible, New International Version®. Copyright © 1973, 1978, 1984 by International Bible Society. Used by permission of Zondervan Publishing House. All rights reserved. Other Scripture references from the *King James Version* (KJV) of the Holy Bible.

Editor: Liz Duckworth
Senior Editor: Janet L. Lee
Cover and Interior design: Dana Sherrer, iDesignEtc.

Library of Congress Cataloging-in-Publication Data
Sims, Barbara.
   Golden wisdom for today's woman : treasured portraits of faith / by
Barbara Sims.
      p. cm.
   ISBN 0-7814-3469-6
1. Vocation--Christianity. I. Title.
   BV4580 .S56 2003
   248.5'43--dc21   2002009002

You may contact the author with comments about this book, or to obtain information on her speaking ministry, *Celebrate!* at:

4913 Brooke Court
Mobile, Alabama 36618

FAX: (251) 343-7770

Dedicated to the memory of

Ella Mae Cheeseman Dossett

who shared with me her time and her golden wisdom.

Acknowledgments

My heartfelt gratitude to:

Fifteen dear women who allowed me to enter their homes, enter their hearts, and display their portraits of wisdom in golden frames.

My agent, Linda Glasford, who fell in love with each of the women and found a home for their stories.

Don, my husband of forty-five years, who instinctively knows when to offer support and encouragement and when to ignore my tears and step over stacks of manuscript revisions without uttering a word.

Margery, my friend, who has walked beside me through five years of writing three (and one-third) books always wielding her monstrous pen that drips red ink. Without that pen, her skillful editing, and even more importantly her constant encouragement to push forward, *Golden Wisdom for Today's Woman* would not have been birthed. Thank you Margery!

Contents

Foreword

The rusty chains of the porch swing squeaked in rhythmical slow motion as two women, one seasoned with wisdom, one young and yearning, celebrated the first breath of spring. The younger woman watched her child play nearby. Idle chatter turned to more meaningful dialogue as the older woman skillfully wove words of wisdom into this often repeated scene. On some days the conversation was philosophical but more often it was simply practical—wisdom for marriage, rearing children, and walking in the light of His love. I was the blessed younger woman. Mrs. Ella Mae Dossett was my mentor.

The changing sands of the twentieth century made porch swings into relics and leisurely morning chats non-existent. Godly women do remain but a twentieth-first century lifestyle leaves little time and few opportunities for today's young woman to sit at the feet of older women—to absorb wisdom gleaned from decades of living a life of faith.

As I reflected on this pattern of changes, I realized my own life is but a composite of what I have gleaned from Mrs. Dossett and countless other women of faith. I wondered who might be today's woman of wisdom. Is she a Sunday school teacher who has taught thirty years and continues to teach the same class today? Is she the widow on my church pew who never misses a service and always offers an encouraging word? The missions matriarch enlisting young women to minister to others?

Or, perhaps, a next-door neighbor who rises early for a quiet time with her Master?

I sought these godly women, found them, and visited in their homes. I listened to their stories. They are ordinary, yet extraordinary women, with ages of seventy-five to ninety-five years. Their reluctance to talk about themselves displayed humility; their life stories revealed faith, compassion, perseverance, and discernment.

My life shall never be the same. I had the opportunity to sit at their feet and listen as fifteen women spoke wisdom from their heart. The golden wisdom found on the following pages comes to you from those women, my fifteen new "friends." Come with me into their homes. Sit with me at their feet. Listen to their hearts. May their wisdom bless your life as it has mine.

Barbara Sims

Helen Marie
A Portrait of Faith

"Trust in the LORD with all thine heart;
and lean not unto thine own understanding.
In all thy ways acknowledge him, and he shall direct thy paths."

(Proverbs 3:5-6, KJV)

*D*ressed as neatly as the patio homes in the neighborhood, Helen Marie, sporting a lime green shirt and matching printed silk pants, answers the ring of her doorbell. I lean down to hug her diminutive body and am greeted by an unidentifiable, sweet, grandmotherly fragrance.

Helen Marie, named after an aunt, was born November 30, 1925, in Philadelphia, Pennsylvania. Her early life was influenced by three women: a grandmother from whom she learned patience and gentleness, her own mother who nursed her in love through two episodes of a life-threatening illness, and a Christian aunt who demonstrated life's most important dimension: spirituality.

Early each Sunday morning Aunt Clara pulled into the driveway at the Buchter home. Helen Marie, in Sunday attire, awaited her ride to church. Aunt Clara was a faithful Sunday School teacher at the Third Brethren Church. "Uncle Harry wasn't regular in attendance," Helen Marie relates. "But one Sunday, after hearing a sermon and not wanting to be left behind, he accepted Christ, became a faithful member, and served as a greeter in the church for many years." This uncle displayed compassion during the depression when he shared resources with Helen Marie's family by paying the family's mortgage notes and keeping the home fires burning.

Aunt Clara and Uncle Harry watched as Helen Marie, at eight years of age, accepted Christ. The entire family followed, also making personal commitments. As was the custom of that church, each person was baptized facing forward and immersed three times, once in the name of the Father, then in the name of the Son, and also the Holy Spirit.

As we continue our visit, Helen Marie's face glows as vibrantly as the bright colors of her clothing. She describes the change that took place in her life as she attended and participated in church activities. But her countenance darkens as she adds, "I was faithful, but faith came much later. There is a difference between faith and faithfulness, you know."

The sixteen-year-old Helen first heard from a young church usher that his friend was going to ask her out. Five years of courtship led them to the altar and an exchange of wedding vows on February 8, 1947. Helen Marie married Johnny Gault, her lifelong love and friend who affectionately called her "Hudge."

The young couple lived with the Buchter family. Johnny worked at Pioneer Paper Company. The money they saved was used to purchase their first home. They welcomed Craig, a child the doctors said they would never bear. Amid child rearing, decorating a new house, and Craig's sports activities, church remained central to family life.

"Those were good years," Helen says with a half-sigh of fond remembrance. But she explains that the couple knew in their hearts they were not living by faith.

Empty business-size envelopes labeled to designate household expenses lined the dining table each payday. Crisp bills, even pocket change, disappeared before their eyes as money was tucked inside to cover "Mortgage Payment," "Groceries," "Gasoline," and other necessities. The last envelope, labeled "Tithe," was left empty every Friday afternoon.

Life was good, but Helen Marie sensed that Johnny was restless. He dreamed of starting his own waste paper business. An offer came from an established company to open a business in Mobile, Alabama. The family migrated south from Hatboro, Pennsylvania to Mobile Bay in south Alabama, known previously as only a dot on a map. Parents, the twelve-year-old son, and a puppy traveled over a thousand miles in a car without air-conditioning through sweltering Southern summer heat and humidity. They purchased a house and found a church in Mobile. The family had found a new home.

Today Helen Marie reminisces about that session she had with God, as she knelt beside her corduroy chair thirty-five years ago. The time and place still have sacred meaning to her.

With two mortgage payments due each month (the home in Pennsylvania had not sold) and living expenses, the couple, though faithful for many years, stepped out on faith. It was a time of recommitment, trusting God's promise to provide for His children. It was time to rearrange the envelopes. The couple vowed to practice what they believed to be scriptural tithing. The envelope marked "Tithe" was the first to be filled each week. They began to practice a higher level of faith and remained faithful in Christian service.

Just as Moses and the Children of Israel encountered problems, Johnny and Helen Marie also experienced difficulties in their "promised land." As the family left church one Sunday morning a devastating call came from an employee. Fire was consuming their business, Hershman—Southern, Incorporated. By night it had burned to the ground, perhaps the work of an arsonist. Helen Marie did the only thing she knew to do. She knelt beside her orange corduroy chair and prayed: "Lord, I have not been completely sold out to you, but I want to be. I am placing complete faith in you today."

"It was this faith," she emphasizes, "that sustained me as we rebuilt the business only to have major contracts canceled. The same faith sustained me when Johnny had his first heart attack prior to his fiftieth birthday and when we moved my aging parents to Mobile. Faith kept me going as I cared for my father dying with Alzheimer's and when my mother lost her battle with congestive heart failure. It also got me through the loss of Johnny." After battling twenty years of congestive heart failure, Helen's Johnny succumbed to a third heart attack at age sixty-four.

Today Helen Marie reminisces about that session she had with God, as she knelt beside her corduroy chair thirty-five years ago. The time and place still have sacred meaning to her. They symbolize the day she began walking down unfamiliar roads, hand in hand with God, in total faith.

I wonder how many lives Helen Marie's has touched with her golden thread of faith. My mind flashes back twenty years. I think about the first time I heard about this remarkable woman. Raye, my friend, shared with me how her life was changed one day in a grocery store, the day she met Helen Marie.

Raye shares that same story with you.

> *"Helen Marie was on a mission when she stood in the line*
> *at my register to pay for a grocery purchase she probably did*

not need. She introduced herself and invited me to visit her church and the Sunday School class of sixteen-year-old girls she taught. Her enthusiasm for her church and her interest in me were genuine. After visiting her Sunday School class, I joined her church. This was the beginning of a relationship that would last a lifetime.

"I have learned so much from Helen Marie. Some lessons were deliberate and overt: how to set the perfect table or how to tie the perfect bow. Many lessons were subtle. I watched her life: the way she interacted with family, friends, and even acquaintances and strangers. She, without realizing that she was the teacher, taught me about forgiveness, generosity, sacrifice, fortitude, and faith.

"There are some people who cross our paths, and in crossing, change our lives forever. Fortunately, for me, our lives blended tightly. Today, more than thirty years later, we walk together and I have been blessed to know her. I have been abundantly blessed to call her my friend."

Now, Helen Marie's path takes her down other unfamiliar

roads. Rheumatic fever, her childhood illness, left her own heart damaged. When I ask her to comment on her uncertain future, she emphasizes, "Today I question nothing. When I go in for scheduled heart procedures, I have peace. Sometimes I can still hear Johnny saying, 'Hudge, just trust.' So I face every day with peace, with faith, just trusting."

I listen and I think: what a testimony! What a difference I could make—or what a difference you could make—if each of us captured this golden vision, walked closely beside our Savior, and faced each day with peace and faith, just trusting.

Helen Marie's
Favorite Scripture Passage

PSALM 121 (KJV)

A Song of degrees.

I will lift up mine eyes unto the hills,

from whence cometh my help.

My help cometh from the LORD,

which made heaven and earth.

He will not suffer thy foot to be moved:

he that keepeth thee will not slumber.

Behold, he that keepeth Israel

shall neither slumber nor sleep.

The LORD is thy keeper:

the LORD is thy shade upon thy right hand.

The sun shall not smite thee by day,

nor the moon by night.

The LORD shall preserve thee from all evil:

he shall preserve thy soul.

The LORD shall preserve thy going out and thy coming in

from this time forth, and even forevermore.

A Recipe From Helen Marie's Kitchen

Sausage Dressing

Three days before dressing is to be eaten, cube three loaves of white bread. Place in roasting pan, uncovered, to dry.

Sauté three cups chopped celery and one and one-half cups chopped onions in a stick of butter. Lightly pan-fry three pounds Jimmy Dean mild sausage.

Mix bread, sausage and drippings, celery and onions. Chop fresh parsley, and mix in bread mixture. Add salt, pepper, and poultry seasoning to taste. May refrigerate until stuffing turkey or bake uncovered.

NOTE FROM HELEN MARIE: Three generations have prepared this recipe for Thanksgiving and Christmas dinners.

Audrey
A Portrait of Faithfulness

"Who can find a virtuous woman?
For her price is far above rubies."

(Proverbs 31:10, KJV)

I am welcomed into the beauty of Audrey's living room. It is a cozy space filled with a collection of dainty prettiness, a term that also aptly describes her. I pause for a moment to enjoy my surroundings, but she encourages me to move to the kitchen. "We are going to sit in here. I want you to see my altar," she says. As we enter the kitchen, I survey the room looking for a place she might kneel, a place she might call her altar.

Audrey points to her table. "This table is more than one-hundred years old." She speaks as if she is savoring its history privately. "I ate at this table with my parents at mealtime. Later I studied the Bible with Jack sitting right here," she says, pointing to the chair she still calls Jack's place. Now Audrey spends two hours every morning sitting here alone studying the Bible.

Simultaneously listening, writing, and thinking, I realize I have found an important constant in our present throwaway world. This table, a part of the past and present, and still anticipating a future, has offered food for body and soul to five generations of Audrey's family. I silently consider the wisdom that must be stored in every fiber of its wood.

Much too quickly Audrey directs my attention to the fading photograph on the den wall that displays a huge, red brick plantation house. She explains it was once surrounded by a barn, smokehouse, and other small buildings. In this house, midway between Jefferson and Winder in a Georgia county called Barrow at that time, Audrey was born to Inez and Albert Foster. The year was 1915 and the massive oak pedestal table arrived later. It was passed from Aunt Celestia to

"We are going to sit in here. I want you to see my altar," she says. As we enter the kitchen, I survey the room looking for a place she might kneel, a place she might call her altar.

her sister, Inez, during Audrey's youth and was the place her family gathered three times each day to give thanks, teach table manners, eat meals, and share their love.

With no school nearby, Audrey spent weekdays with Grandmother Miranda and Grandfather Henry near Winder. She left the family home each Monday in a buggy driven by Aunt Ruth (also a student) and pulled by faithful Charlie, the family horse. They returned each Friday afternoon.

On weekends another, and even more important, education was ensured as Albert took his family to church. Here they joined with friends and neighbors in Christian worship, and it was here that each child made his or her personal commitment to Christ.

Described by a family member as "a mere wisp of a girl at age sixteen," Audrey met Jack at that very church. Eight years her senior, Jack was considered an older man. When they began to date, her family, especially her father, expressed concern about the age difference. Dating, Audrey explains, was "walking home after church at night holding hands." The couple married two years after they met. "There was little cause for my father's concern," Audrey volunteers, "for during our sixty years of marriage Jack always behaved as if he adored me."

Their married life was a saga of three churches—First Baptist Church of Citronelle, Toulminville Baptist Church, and Moffett Road Baptist Church, each located in Mobile County, Alabama. Jack and Audrey were involved in a multitude of church activities, from teaching Sunday School, working in Training Union, and promoting missions, to playing the piano and singing in the choir— even locking up the church after services. One memorable Sunday

She sent the girls out to invite neighborhood children to backyard Bible study. Audrey sat under the trees each morning, with children at her feet, reading Bible storybooks, words some neighborhood children had never heard.

night the couple returned to their car and counted only two of their three boys.

"Where's Charles?" Audrey asked. The couple quickly retrieved baby Charles. He was inside the locked church—asleep in the nursery!

At home, life was centered on the oak table as a second

generation, the parents and three sons—Brantley, Foster, and Charles—shared meals, laughed, cried, and nourished bodies, minds, and souls. And it was around this table many years later that Audrey gathered visiting grandchildren to learn Bible verses on hot summer afternoons.

A now grown-up grandson remembers how he was called from outside fun during summer visits to sit at the oak table and memorize Scriptures. Not always happy then about the interruptions, Brant credits his grandmother for much of the Scripture he quotes from memory today, verses he learned at this table.

However, all teaching did not happen inside around the table, nor was it limited to family. Audrey insisted that all the grandchildren come simultaneously to visit each summer. She sent the girls out to invite neighborhood children to backyard Bible study. Audrey sat under the trees each morning, with children at her feet, reading Bible storybooks, words some neighborhood children had never heard.

Audrey adores her grandchildren, but her thoughts often return to her beloved Jack. "We were married sixty-six years," she muses. "His death came after a long struggle with leukemia."

My mind drifts as I wonder, How does one survive the death of a spouse after more than half a century of marriage?

As if reading my thoughts, Audrey begins to speak softly, allowing me an almost too-private glimpse of her precious relationship with Jack, as well as the depth of her personal relationship with God.

"Jack loved life more than anyone I have ever known. I knew he was dying. We kissed and he kissed me right back, and I knew it was the end. And it was. I knew that life would never be the same, but I still had the Lord to depend on. I prayed, 'Lord, I don't know if I can do this.' His answer came immediately that I could meet this challenge, with His help."

It has been nine years since Jack's death. Audrey says she still puts her foot on Jack's side of the bed, the same place where his foot rested during six decades of marriage. "It give me comfort," she explains. "But my strength comes from God."

Audrey remains faithful today. After teaching Sunday School for sixty-six years, she now serves as a secretary and still sings in the choir at Moffett Road Baptist Church. And she meets her Master at that same oak table early every morning in Bible study.

"When I am finished with study I move to my altar to pray," she adds. I sense that she will tell me about the altar only when she is ready.

I inquire about the large stack of books lying on the table. "This is what I am using for Bible study," Audrey explains. "This my Bible, Sunday School quarterly, and *Open Windows*, a devotional book." Audrey uses all her strength to lift a thick, hardcover book, *The Complete Parallel Bible*. She says, "I'm in First Chronicles in the Old Testament and Hebrews in the New Testament. It's slow, but I work on it every day." The extensive study Bible was a birthday gift from her son Charles and his family on her eighty-fifth birthday.

"This is where I lift my heart in prayer for my family. I stand right here at the refrigerator to pray each morning when I finish my Bible study. I point to these pictures and I pray for children, grandchildren, great-grandchildren and spouses. I pray at my altar every day."

Finally Audrey directs my attention to her altar. Dozens,

perhaps hundreds, of pictures of family members—children, grandchildren, great-grandchildren, and spouses—neatly adorn her refrigerator. "This is my altar," she says. "This is where I lift my heart in prayer for my family. I stand right here at the refrigerator to pray each morning when I finish my Bible study. I point to these pictures and I pray for children, grandchildren, great-grandchildren and spouses. I pray at my altar every day."

Faithful, I think. Faithful in marriage, family, churches, Bible study, and in daily prayer—at her altar.

Audrey is "Mama Audie," "Maudie," or more often just "Audie" to three sons, nine grandchildren and twenty great-grandchildren. Recently they gathered to honor her, a faithful woman, on a special day, her eighty-fifth birthday. Daughter-in-law Joanne spoke the sentiments of family and all those who know her:

"We are a fortunate family.

'Who can find a virtuous woman?'

We can. Her name is Audrey."

Audrey's Favorite Hymn

GREAT IS THY FAITHFULNESS

Thomas O. Chisholm

Great is Thy faithfulness, O God my Father,
There is no shadow of turning with Thee;
Thou changest not, Thy compassions, they fail not;
As Thou hast been Thou forever wilt be.

Summer and winter, and springtime and harvest,
Sun, moon, and stars in their courses above,
Join with all nature in manifold witness
To Thy great faithfulness, mercy, and love.

Pardon for sin and a peace that endureth,
Thy own dear presence to cheer and to guide;
Strength for today and bright hope for tomorrow,
Blessings all mine, with ten thousand beside!

CHORUS:

Great is Thy faithfulness! Great is Thy faithfulness!
Morning by morning new mercies I see;
All I have needed Thy hand hath provided;
Great is Thy faithfulness! Lord unto me!

A Recipe From Audie's Kitchen

HOT CHICKEN SALAD

2 cups stewed chicken, chopped

1 cup celery, diced

3 hard-boiled eggs, diced

1/2 cup mayonnaise

1 can cream of chicken soup

1 can water chestnuts

Salt and pepper to taste

Potato chips, crushed

Mix all ingredients, except potato chips. Put in a two-quart casserole and cover with potato chips. Bake for 20 minutes at 400 degrees. Serves six.

NOTE FROM AUDIE: Prepare, refrigerate, and cook later for 45 minutes or until heated thoroughly.

Eugenia
A Portrait of Discernment

"Better one handful with tranquillity
than two handfuls with toil and chasing after the wind."

(Ecclesiastes 4:6, NIV)

Sixteen youngsters crowded together in a small Andalusia, Alabama, schoolroom early one morning in 1930. Eight of the students were fourth graders who had achieved the highest scores on the Stanford Binet test administered the previous year; the other eight were third graders who had not been promoted to the fourth grade the year before. It was a banner day for each child present. The group had been chosen to participate in the "Opportunity Classroom." This pilot program was an educational experiment under the guidance of a master teacher, Elsa Lundquist, a young Swedish woman with a master's degree from Columbia University.

In addition to completing their own fourth grade work, eight children became tutors to those needing academic assistance. And in return, those needing tutoring shared their strengths. One child taught a schoolmate to crochet, and another successfully demonstrated to uncoordinated Eugenia the art of jumping rope.

Benefits from this unique opportunity were obvious. The group who served as tutors completed two grades that year with time left for the pursuit of individual interests and projects. Most students in the group needing academic assistance reached grade level.

Within the walls of the Opportunity Room this future teacher learned about compassion. She began to realize that everyone has value and worth. And it was here that she learned to love learning.

Some rewards were less tangible but no less meaningful. For Eugenia the classroom was a happy, magical retreat. Within the walls of the Opportunity Room this future teacher learned about compassion. She began to realize that everyone has value and worth. And it was here that she learned to love learning.

Eugenia was born the first child to an attorney father—whom she loved completely and wanted to please—and a creative mother, who was both a schoolteacher and gardener. "My mother was intelligent and full of wit. She appreciated beautiful things and was a talented painter," Eugenia says. She directs my attention to an exquisite painting on her living room wall, a cabin in the woods surrounded by snow. The lively color of Eugenia's dress and the glow of her face and voice appear momentarily to mesh with the painting—a gift of love, a legacy left by her mother.

The beautiful word pictures Eugenia shares about her early life are soon replaced by descriptions of dark pain she experienced at the tender age of seven, when her mother died from complications following the birth of her stillborn child. Three years after her mother's death Eugenia stood beside another coffin. Only forty-three years old, her beloved father died from a sudden heart attack while attending a Thanksgiving Day football game.

Poignant glimpses of that time remain indelible in her memory. She overheard someone at the wake saying, "Doesn't he look natural?" The ten-year-old thought, *No, he doesn't. The light has gone out.* She also recalls realizing at this early age that nothing in life is certain.

After her father's funeral Eugenia and her sister were taken to Mobile in the middle of the night by maternal grandparents. Living in the home of her minister grandfather, educated and intelligent, but strict and old-fashioned, was not the environment the hurting child needed for healing. She was bewildered by the discrepancy between his devotion to his God and his frequent, harsh judgment of those who did not share his views—biblical or otherwise. Yet, sympathy for him led her to go forward during a revival service when no one responded. "This was no salvation experience," she explains. "I felt sorry for my grandfather and he dipped me in water, but I had no faith at the time. When you are a child and both parents die, you wonder where God is. You wonder why God allows bad things to happen if He is in control."

I ponder this extreme hurt, the death of both mother and father followed by disillusion. I wonder how a mere child of ten could survive such trauma to become the person of faith sitting across the room.

As if she hears my thoughts, Eugenia continues. "I wouldn't want you to think there was no happiness in my early life. I have fond memories of loving parents, friends, and teachers—many happy memories. I had advantages others did not have. My father provided for my college education before his death. And these were the Depression years. These experiences, like all of life's suffering—we cannot afford to waste such an expenditure of feelings—we have to learn from it. We have to find the gift in it."

As Eugenia continues I wonder how many gifts I may have missed when I failed to learn from my own difficult circumstances.

Following a court battle between her father's family and her mother's family, Eugenia returned to familiar surroundings, her family residence. Here her paternal grandmother cared for her. "Never once in my life did I hear her say an unkind word," Eugenia says. "She was uneducated and frugal to a fault, yet generous. She would have given you the shirt off her back."

> *These experiences, like all of life's suffering—we cannot afford to waste such an expenditure of feelings—we have to learn from it. We have to find the gift in it."*

Two spare bedrooms were rented to an assortment of women: teachers, a social worker, and once the county nurse. To Eugenia's delight, Miss Lunquist, her classroom teacher in the Opportunity Room was the first roomer. This beloved teacher was addressed at school as "Miss Lunquist" but at home she was known as Aunt Elsa.

"This 'Guardian Angel' took me under her wing for the three years she lived with us," Eugenia says as she continues her story. "She was certainly a mastermind at requiring one to examine different points of view. She was a loving, nurturing woman but also a strict, plainspoken one. She would not tolerate self-pity or excuses."

I realize I am sitting across the room from one who speaks forthrightly, a person devoid of hypocrisy, true to herself and others. She is a thinker; she is discerning, unassuming, and kind, all qualities taught by her teacher by day and displayed in the classroom of life during evening hours.

Eugenia's heart was touched when she spent a week at a lakeside youth retreat. A young minister from Anniston, Charles Bell, different from anyone she had ever heard, preached about a God who loved her. "This was the first time I heard a preacher talk about love. This was when I truly put my faith in God—where I began a journey of faith." That faith has been lived out and is evident in her life today, more than sixty years later.

"We only become aware of who we really are when we are about thirty years old," Eugenia says. "We realize what matters, and it is not things. I spent a lot of energy wanting things I could not afford before I learned what is important—family, friends, and the contribution one can make.

"In fact, I think each of us is a 'work in progress.' I am a Christian who happens to be a Baptist. Since this is my path, Christ, as revealed in the Bible, is my authority. But there are some things we don't understand in this lifetime. There are ambiguities. I see God's qualities expressed by Christ. Christ is the measure. I am on the road and I use Jesus as the plumb line. The test of real religion is if its followers behave with compassion and responsibility toward others. We can't be everything to everybody but each one of us can do something.

"Also, I do consider my faith the soil in which I am rooted. But I find it difficult to talk about it—maybe because it is the result of so many struggles and . . . " Displaying deep humility she adds, "I have so far to go to be worthy of God's grace."

Eugenia then reaches deep into the secret pockets of her life as she shares with me her written journal, filled with gems she has read and collected and her own profound original thoughts—"nuggets of gold"—she has mined over many years. One piece of wealth, a reflection and composite of her life, rings loud and clear for everyone, but especially those who have experienced shattered dreams and heavy hearts....

"It is not happiness that makes us grow, rather it is challenge."

Eugenia's Favorite Hymn

IMMORTAL, INVISIBLE, GOD ONLY WISE

Walter Chalmers Smith

Immortal, invisible, God only wise,

In light inaccessible hid from our eyes,

Most blessed, most glorious, the Ancient of Days,

Almighty, victorious, Thy great name we praise.

Unresting, unhasting, and silent as light,

Nor wanting, nor wasting, Thou rulest in might;

Thy justice like mountains high soaring above,

Thy clouds which are fountains of goodness and love.

To all life Thou givest—to both great and small;

In all life Thou livest, the true life of all;

We blossom and flourish, like leaves on the tree,

And wither and perish—but, naught changeth Thee.

Great Father of Glory, pure Father of light,

Thine angels adore Thee, all veiling their sight;

All laud we would render: O help us to see

'Tis only the splendor of light hideth Thee!

A Recipe From Eugenia's Kitchen

COMPANY BEEF TENDERLOIN

Marinade: 3 oz. soy sauce
1 oz. Kitchen Bouquet
1 oz. Worcestershire sauce

Marinate any size beef tenderloin in refrigerator 8 hours or overnight. (I use a large Ziplock plastic bag.) Turn meat until marinade coats all sides.

Remove tenderloin from refrigerator in time for it to reach room temperature before cooking.

Heat oven to 450 degrees.

Place tenderloin on a rack in an uncovered pan and put in heated oven.

For medium rare: Cook meat for 22 minutes; turn off oven and leave for 15-17 minutes. Do not open oven during this time.

For medium done: Cook meat for 23-24 minutes; turn off oven and leave 15-17 minutes. Do not open the oven during this time.

Evelyn
A Portrait of Love

---·◆·---

"God is love;
and he that dwelleth in love dwelleth in God,
and God in him."

(1 John 4:16b, KJV)

"*I*s one name adequate to describe the greatness of God?" Evelyn asks the rhetorical question while describing her latest adventure in the Scriptures, her own quiet quest for a closer walk, and a deeper relationship with God.

"I am studying the wonderful names of God," the eighty-four-year-old explains. "Years ago I studied the names of God from a book. After searching fruitlessly for that book I began my study early this year, using the Scriptures and Kay Arthur's book *Lord, I Want to Know You*. But one day as I reached for something else, I found my hands on the book—*Names of God*, by Nathan Stone, the very book I studied earlier."

Evelyn's sweet voice recites in soft awe, "Creator, Lord, Almighty, Provider, Master. These are some of the names used in the Scriptures that offer believers deeper insight into the majesty of God."

I listen intently, savoring each tender word. I visualize the serenity of her face, even though we are speaking by telephone. I knew she was special when I met her last November. You see, Evelyn walks closely beside this one she calls Master.

The fall foliage on either side of the car defined for me a narrow dirt road. We crept forward on bumpy, unfamiliar territory as I followed directions read to me by copilot, Mabel. Less than two miles from a major U.S. highway, the road abruptly ended in the front yard of a lovely country home. It was in this quiet setting, surrounded by nature, that my friend Mabel introduced me to her longtime friend, Evelyn.

Born to loving parents, Evelyn had happy childhood experiences. She relates warm memories of family times: taking piano lessons, playing the violin in her high school orchestra, and making a commitment to Christ at an early age. "My family gave me a foundation for living and fertile soil for Christian growth following my salvation experience." Though she was born in Ellisville, Mississippi, Evelyn soon moved with her family to Mobile, Alabama. After marrying, Evelyn and Albert gravitated toward the suburbs of Mobile and eventually settled in this rural Eden.

Life was busy for the couple as they reared four children— three sons and a daughter. But Evelyn, an avid reader, always found time to study the Scriptures and read inspirational material. "Reading propels one forward," she offers. "Then God honors our efforts and we grow more like Christ. I read somewhere that as Christians we should always be *looking*, *longing*, and *loving*."

ALWAYS LOOKING

The ever-present glow about her face intensifies as afternoon sun filters through the living room window. Evelyn's search included light inspirational writers such as Joyce Landorf, Anita Bryant, Catherine Marshall, as well as the deeper spiritual material of Louise Eggleston, Scott Peck, Charles Spugeon, and others. A favorite author, Frances Ridley Havergal, also wrote, "Take My Life," the words of Evelyn's favorite hymn. Music has also spoken to her heart. Ministers have given godly direction. Friendships have provided examples for growth.

Evelyn pauses for a moment and turns toward our friend. "Mabel has always been an encourager. I think I have learned something from every person I have ever met," she muses. "God sends people and experiences to help us grow but only when we are ready to learn."

In my own mind and heart, I wonder, am I ready to learn?

Always open for instruction, always turning toward her Savior, Evelyn is *looking* and *longing*.

ALWAYS LONGING

"My desire is to spend every day in a spirit of prayer. For many years I met my Master at daybreak on the back patio," Evelyn said. "It's something I began more than thirty years ago. My husband left early for work. The first light of daybreak was calming. Each morning I felt the serene presence of God. I have used the peaceful settings of our woods and lake for times of worship."

Recollections of intimate times in the presence of God, perhaps not previously shared, are humbly whispered. Burdened in years past while rearing teenagers, she prayed earnestly, and then ended her prayer by speaking aloud, "Lord, I don't know what to do!" As if she had heard an audible voice from the other side of a nearby door, the answer came: "Fear not." Only two words, but Evelyn felt her burden lifted.

Now the couple is on a retirement schedule but the longing remains; perhaps, it is even stronger. The Bible study and prayer time at the feet of her Master continue during a short midmorning time and for several hours later in the evening.

Evelyn remains *looking, longing,* and LOVING.

ALWAYS LOVING

One has only to be in her presence to feel surrounded by love. The constant smile, a warm welcome for a stranger who came into her home, and the special "tea time" she planned to refresh us during the interview are outward manifestations of Evelyn's inner quality—love.

As she shared painful life experiences, I began to understand how strongly love controls her behavior. When a crisis arises, Evelyn first asks herself the question, "What is my role in this situation?"

I realize I am in the presence of one whose life is truly controlled by love. She is willing to be involved, and there is no hint of a selfish motive. I am distracted as I admit in my heart that many of my own decisions are not made in this spirit of love.

I know this loving spirit surely has touched many lives. I want a story, an example, or word picture to touch the hearts of those who are not privileged to sit in her home.   But I sense the answer before I ask the question. Her reply, "If I have ever touched the life of another person, I am not aware of it."

> "*If* my life has made an impression on anyone, it is because with that person's heart's eye, I have been seen leaning on my Master."

"Tell, me a story," I plead, "about someone who wrote a note to thank you for something that touched him or her."

After a too long silence, she replies. "If my life has made an impression on anyone, it is because with that person's heart's eye, I have been seen leaning on my Master." She pauses as if struggling for words.

"There was a child at the elementary school; Pam was her

name ... She wrote me a letter ... We became pen pals ... She moved away." I am almost afraid to ask. "Do you know where she is ... how to get in touch with her?" An address is secured, a letter mailed, a telephone call made to a distant city, and I allow the grown-up Pam to tell her love story.

PAM'S STORY

"I don't know how I knew, but I knew she was different.

"Mrs. Allen was a teacher's aide at Wilmer School. She was precious to me. She always acted like she cared about me. I don't remember many specifics but I knew she loved me.

"When I was in the sixth grade Mrs. Allen retired. Some of her former students presented a schoolwide play in her honor, thanking her "just for being you." I was chosen to be "Mrs. Allen." On the party day I wore a gray wig to school, a navy blue skirt, and a white blouse. Mrs. Allen arrived dressed just like me!

"Several years later I wrote a letter to her and asked if we could be pen pals. She answered my letter, and we have corresponded for almost twenty years.

"When I graduated from high school she gave me a book for

graduation, Wisdom for the Graduate. We always wrote—not every week—but we keep in touch. Everything she writes is an encouragement to my faith. I moved to Georgia to live with my sister who had found Christ as Savior. My sister introduced me to Christ and, perhaps, it was then that I began to understand the love I saw displayed in Mrs. Allen's life. Later, when I returned to Alabama to visit, I went to her home. It was a special time—she served tea outside in dainty cups.

"My husband and I were childless for nine years. One Sunday night our pastor asked the church to surround us and pray at the end of a Sunday evening service. In a few weeks I knew. We were going to have that longed-for child! Before our son, Ryan, was two years old, we became foster parents to twins—Shelby and Sheila. I knew the girls and their family. I had taken the children to church. I got a call late one night. Their mother had been killed in an automobile accident. My husband and I applied to be foster parents. We were approved and before the twins came to live with us , I was pregnant with our daughter, Allison.

"After all these years, marrying, active in church, moving through life, we have kept in touch. Mrs. Allen remains my role model, my encourager, my pen pal."

I held in my hand the Christmas card mailed to Evelyn from Pam in December, 1999. Pam's handwritten words may best describe how God used this loving woman:

"To Mrs. Allen,

One who really touched the life of a child.

Merry Christmas from Pam,

The child you touched forever."

When Evelyn shares with me the story she learned through letters over the years and I learned by long-distance telephone, I remind her again that she had touched Pam's life in a dramatic way. Her reply? "I suppose God sometimes uses rusty old pipes as channels for His blessings."

Surely, I think, He has used the life of this woman who has spent a lifetime looking, longing, and loving.

But rusty old pipes? Maybe. Perhaps, then, He could use even my life to touch others.

Evelyn's Favorite Hymn

TAKE MY LIFE AND LET IT BE

Francis R. Havergal

Take my life, and let it be
Consecrated, Lord, to Thee;
Take my hands, and let them move
At the impulse of Thy love,
At the impulse of Thy love.

Take my feet, and let them be
Swift and beautiful for Thee;
Take my voice, and let me sing
Always, only, for my King,
Always, only, for my King.

Take my will and make it Thine;
It shall be no longer mine;
Take my heart, it is Thine own!
It shall be Thy royal throne,

Chorus:

Lord, I give my life to Thee,
Thine forever more to be;
Lord, I give my life to Thee,
Thine forevermore to be.

A Recipe From Evelyn's Kitchen

BROCCOLI CORNBREAD

1 package Jiffy corn muffin mix

1 medium onion, chopped

2 cups cheese, grated

4 eggs and a dash of salt

1 stick margarine, melted

1 package frozen chopped broccoli, thawed and drained well

Mix well. Pour into an 11 x 7-inch pan sprayed with cooking oil.

Bake at 350 degrees for 40 minutes or until done.

Burma
A Portrait of Strength

"Let not your heart be troubled: ye believe in God, believe also in me. In my Father's house are many mansions: if it were not so, I would have told you. I go to prepare a place for you. And if I go and prepare a place for you, I will come again, and receive you unto myself; that where I am, there ye may be also."

(John 14:1-3, KJV)

*T*n Keesler Military Hospital, miles from home, his wife, three adult children, and their families, dealt with Tom's impending death. The nurse entered the room, stood quietly, then took Burma by the hand and led her to a hallway outside the room. She whispered compassionately to the weeping wife, "You must let him go. He is holding on for you."

Burma embraced the nurse then turned and walked through the door to the bedside and led her family in saying good-bye to Tom, her mate of fifty years. "If I could sing you a song, I would send you on your way. You need to … let go. You have fought a good fight and you can go with the assurance that one day each of us will be with you."

Five years had passed since the night Tom slipped quietly into the presence of his Savior. On a blustery December afternoon I park my car under a magnolia tree outside Burma's home in sight of Moffett Road Baptist, her church home. I retreat briefly in my mind to a time when this strong woman mentored me, and then I knock on the front door. Gracious, as always, Burma invites me into her den where she serves tea, cookies, and beautiful stories.

I retreat briefly in my mind to a time when this strong woman mentored me, and then I knock on the front door. Gracious, as always, Burma invites me into her den where she serves tea, cookies, and beautiful stories.

Born into the home of Arris and Ocie Reid, Burma was reared in Jones County, near Laurel, Mississippi. Ocie, the Bethlehem Baptist Church matriarch of missions, taught Sunbeams, the preschool mission program. The church had no mission program for elementary-age girls, so Burma remained in the Sunbeam group until youth age and still today claims the title "oldest Sunbeam."

During the annual "First Week in July Revival Meeting," led by evangelist Gordon Sansing, eleven-year-old Burma gave her heart to Christ. A local school bus provided transportation the following Sunday to nearby Mill Creek where fourteen new converts were baptized. Two years later, young Burma met her future husband, Tom Leggett, seven years her senior. Of course, they didn't date—she was much too young—they just rode the school bus together: Burma, to high school, and Tom, to a nearby college. Nevertheless the wheels of destiny were turning for this couple.

The World War II draft claimed Tom after his second year of college and he was sent to Europe. Although the plane he was piloting was downed by enemy fire, Tom returned in 1945 to U.S. soil to wed Burma. His air force career took the couple and their two young sons back across the Atlantic, as God moved in a dramatic way in the lives of the family and in Burma as an individual.

Her early exposure to missions in Bethlehem Baptist Church

instilled in Burma a lifelong commitment. She was intrigued by the concept of "reaching out unto the ends of the earth." A friend in her youth mission group felt called to Africa to minister. "I was a little jealous when she felt called," Burma admits, "and I wondered why God did not call me to Africa."

Why not Africa? Perhaps, God had another mission plan on foreign soil for Burma—Germany. And perhaps even bigger plans later on home soil.

Tom's two tours of duty in Europe offered Burma opportunities to work with The Protestant Women of the Chapel. "I really got to do missions in Europe," Burma volunteers. "I went into homes and shared the story of Christ, homes with clay floors, stables we would call them. We took Christmas gifts to a young widow whose husband was killed during the war, dolls for the girls and a train for the little boy. Most of the families we ministered to did not speak English. We gave them Christian tracts in their language." Led by Burma as president, the organization had clothes showers for needy families and carried food to homes at Thanksgiving time.

This is missions in action; I think—the golden rule, meeting the needs of others, serving where we are, demonstrating the love of Christ—the heart of the Gospel.

While they were stationed in Germany, God blessed Burma's mission efforts in an unusual way, and He also blessed the Leggett family, Tom, Burma, Tommy, and Richard in a personal way.

During Tom's second tour in Europe a neighbor called and asked to come to the Leggett home to talk to Burma. Burma was not prepared for what she heard. The young German woman shared that she had four older children and a newborn who was still in the hospital nursery. She said she loved her children but wanted to give her newborn daughter to Burma, saying she would not give her to anyone else. Ten days later Barbara Anna was placed in the arms of the Leggett family, fulfilling their longing for a little girl.

She was intrigued by the concept of "reaching out unto the ends of the earth." A friend in her youth mission group felt called to Africa to minister. "I was a little jealous when she felt called," Burma admits, "and I wondered why God did not call me to Africa."

Doing God's will sometimes means waiting patiently. While we wait, we can love God and tell others about Him. Burma views the family's time in Germany as a time of waiting while telling others about Him. It was only after she returned to the States, that she fully realized her personal calling, which she describes simply as a call to pray, to give, and to send.

Burma's zeal for missions and strength of leadership were quickly recognized as she served faithfully and emerged as a leader, both in her church's Women's Missionary Union and in Mobile (County) Baptist Association. She served for four consecutive years as President of Alabama Baptist WMU. It was while serving on the Alabama Women's Missionary Union Executive Board that Burma found herself getting off a plane in Nigeria. As a member of a three-person team she spoke at their convention to Nigerian women through an interpreter. Recalling her earlier jealousy she admitted, "Even though I knew I was called to go, at this stage in my life I was comfortable in not being called to stay." But the trip gave her a new respect for career missionaries, the conditions under which they work, and the challenges they face. Burma returned home strengthened, more committed to pray, to give, and to send.

Her persuasion was strong as she enlisted younger women and challenged them to serve in places of leadership. I know. As a young mother with two children and many church responsibilities, I received a telephone call from Burma, a woman I had not met. She asked me to serve in a position I did not know existed. And I said, yes! This tower of strength mentored me as she marched forward untiringly organizing groups of women to promote missions in their respective churches. I was one of many lives touched as she prayed, gave, sent, and challenged those at home to serve.

The afternoon sun is fading as outside temperatures plummet, yet I am reluctant to leave. As Burma pours our second cup of tea, I thank her for the impact she made on my life more than thirty years ago.

"Oh, Barbara, I am nothing," she replies. "In God's service the greatest ability is accountability. It is not where we walk but with whom we walk with that matters."

I recognize afresh that the strength I so admire in this one is also available to me—but only if I am willing to be accountable and walk closely. I wonder, am I willing? In my heart I pray, God help me to be more willing.

Sitting across from Burma, I nod as she speaks. Our conversation drifts back to family, children, grandchildren, and to Tom, her encourager and soul mate. I ask about the healing process and how she made it through the difficult time after Tom's death. "To be paralyzed by fear is to question God's ability to take care of me," she says. "Only in God's presence are we safe and secure, so I prayed. I wrote my prayers. Writing helped me to survive. God is willing to listen to anything that I want to tell Him. I kept a journal of my prayers for several years."

My heart soars as I consider the possibility of reading the journal. But Burma continues, "I looked for that book recently, and I couldn't find it anywhere."

A few days later Burma finds the journal: outside, a worn, hard plastic cover splashed with multicolored flowers, but inside, private conversations with a personal friend. With Burma's permission I offer to you a glimpse of her pain. Recorded in her diary are prayers collected five years earlier from unknown sources. Burma used these words in intimate conversations with her Source of strength.

"Help me O God, I am tired of this wilderness. Sometimes I think it will never end. I feel so needy that I don't like what I see in the mirror. Are you testing me? If so, what am I supposed to be learning? Help me to cling to you and strengthen me against the temptation of self-pity. Lead me to a place of safety. Amen."

"Father, Thank you for your tender love. When I am tempted to feel alone and abandoned, help me to remember that you are near to watch over me. Amen."

"Dear Lord, Help me to live this day quietly, easily; to lean upon thy strength, waiting for the unfolding of thy will patiently and serenely, to meet others peacefully, joyously; to face tomorrow confidently, courageously. Amen."

The past year has brought new difficulties prompting Burma to cling to golden spiritual strength through prayer. Younger son Richard underwent serious surgery to remove a brain tumor and Tom Jr., a minister, suffered a heart attack. Even as I carefully turn the pages of Burma's journal and prepare to inscribe her conversations with her Lord in this manuscript, I learn from a mutual friend that Tom, Jr. is continuing to have cardiac problems.

Midmorning, two days later I am sitting at my computer when the front doorbell rings. Burma stops by briefly as she is leaving town. She appears shaken and I insist that she come in for a moment. Her pain-filled voice relates, "Tommy is not doing well and I am on my way there. Richard will have surgery again next Tuesday. The brain tumor has recurred. Please pray for us."

Burma joins the list of godly women who face continual and overwhelming occasions of grief. This crisis, like those she has walked through before, becomes a time of prayer, searching, and leaning heavily on the Source of strength—her Lord, her strength and her Redeemer.

Burma's Favorite Hymn

THE LILY OF THE VALLEY

Charles Fry

I have found a friend in Jesus, He's everything to me,
He's the fairest of ten thousand to my soul;
The Lily of the Valley, in Him alone I see
All I need to cleanse and make me fully whole.
In sorrow He's my comfort, in trouble He's my stay;
He tells me every care on Him to roll.
He's the Lily of the Valley, the bright and Morning Star,
He's the fairest of ten thousand to my soul.

He all my griefs has taken, and all my sorrows borne;
In temptation He's my strong and mighty tower;
I have all for Him forsaken, and all my idols torn
From my heart, and now He keeps me by His power.
Though all the world forsake me and Satan tempt me sore,
Through Jesus I shall safely reach the goal.
He's the Lily of the Valley, the bright and Morning Star,
He's the fairest of ten thousand to my soul.

He will never, never leave me nor yet forsake me here,

While I live by faith and do His blessed will;

A wall of fire about me, I've nothing now to fear,

With His manna He my hungry soul shall fill,

Then sweeping up to glory to see His blessed face,

Where rivers of delight shall ever roll.

He's the Lily of the Valley, the bright and Morning Star,

He's the fairest of ten thousand to my soul.

A Recipe From Burma's Kitchen

SHRIMP CREOLE

2 lbs. raw shrimp

3/4 cup onions, chopped

1/2 cup shallots, chopped

1 cup green pepper, chopped

1/2 clove garlic, minced

2 tablespoons butter

1 tablespoon salt

1/8 teaspoon paprika

1/2 teaspoon pepper

1/2 teaspoon oregano

1 pint stewed tomatoes

Sauté onions, shallots, green pepper, and garlic in butter. Let simmer until green pepper is tender. Add other ingredients, except shrimp, and boil for 5 minutes. Add shrimp and boil for 10 minutes. Serve over rice. Serves six.

Leola

A Portrait of Missions

The open-air tabernacle offered overhead protection from morning sun for worshipers sitting on crude wooden benches. Distant clouds and the subtle rumbling of thunder gave hints of a morning shower. In the midst of the woodlands of north Mobile County, voices of all ages meshed with outside sounds of nature to proclaim:

> O Lord my God, when I in awesome wonder,
> Consider all the worlds Thy hands have made,
> I see the stars, I hear the rolling thunder,
> Thy power throughout the universe displayed.

The year was 1961. I was a young mother and volunteer teacher at Family Camp, a Southern Baptist Convention Home Mission outreach to an Indian population known today as the Mowa Tribe. Families spent an entire week at the rustic campground. While husbands were working at jobs during the day, wives and children were participating in craft activities, Bible study, and worship. Each evening husbands joined their families for supper followed by evening worship. Here the Gospel was preached, hearts were touched, and lives changed.

It was in this setting that I first heard the words of the hymn "How Great Thou Art," as the voices of tribal families and volunteer workers blended in enthusiastic praise. And it was here that I met Leola Isbell, a missionary with the Home Mission Board who, along with her husband, worked for thirty years on this south Alabama Indian field.

Leola was born in Stevenville, Texas to Christian parents who were faithful members of a local church pastored by her future father-in-law. The family farmed, borrowing money in the spring to plant crops and repaying the money each fall. Her pattern for life was set as she traveled with her family by wagon to church each Sunday and went forward in a Sunday service to accept Christ as Savior.

"Our pastor talked to us about God's call for each of our lives. I was interested in missions," Leola says. "Growing up I always thought I would be an old maid missionary. After high school I was able to attend Howard Payne College on money collected and given to me by my church for tuition and the 17 dollars I earned each week working at the local Woolworths store.

"I was a part of the first summer mission group sent out by the Southern Baptist Convention. I knew that a missionary was someone who went somewhere else and told others about Jesus. I really didn't understand at the time what it meant to be called. I just knew I was supposed to go."

Our pastor talked to us about God's call for each of our lives. I was interested in missions. I was a part of the first summer mission group sent out by the Southern Baptist Convention. I really didn't understand at the time what it meant to be called. I just knew I was supposed to go.

Distracted for a moment from the interview, I am consumed with my own thoughts. In her youth Leola willingly ventured out on faith simply because she knew she was supposed to go. Instantly I recall missed opportunities in my own life—those times when I wasn't willing to act because I did not feel I had complete understanding.

That summer Leola had the privilege of working in the Indian Center Baptist Church in Oklahoma City under the direction of Victor and Eileen Kaneubee. The church reached people from many tribes and reservations who came to the city to find work. Leola found it interesting that even before asking someone his name, the Indians asked, "What tribe are you?" In worship services each tribe in turn sang in their own tribal language.

After graduation Leola approached Dr. J. B. Rounds, superintendent of the Indian mission, inquiring about a job. He answered, "I don't have a place for single women. Can you get married?"

As a college graduate without immediate marriage prospects, Leola found employment teaching school in a distant state, Alabama. The school was populated by a little known Indian tribe in a place that she would soon call home. She and future husband,

Elbert Isbell, dated by mail while he attended Southwestern Seminary in Fort Worth, Texas. Elbert always teased and told others that she asked him to marry so she could be appointed as a missionary. It was the mailman, not Elbert, who presented the engagement ring, mailed from Texas and delivered via mail to Leola in Alabama.

After Elbert's seminary graduation and their wedding, the couple established their home in the area where Leola was teaching. He pastored churches and served as an associational missionary. When the home missionary to the area, John Issacs, retired in 1957, he approached Elbert and Leola about applying to serve on the South Alabama Indian Field. After submitting their personal testimonies and a recommendation from Rev. Issacs, the couple was appointed by the Home Mission Board of the Southern Baptist Convention to serve as missionaries to the Indian tribe in south Alabama.

"They never told us what to do," Leola explains. "We were just given responsibility to become catalysts—to make things happen that would touch the hearts and lives of this unique Indian group not yet recognized by the United States government."

Elbert and Leola (with sons Glenn and Joe, and infant daughter Elaine) immersed themselves in a different culture and a challenging assignment. Recognizing that many missionaries face this transition, I inquire about the secret of their long and effective work.

"It was not always easy teaching the Christian lifestyle," she says. "I recall the time when a church member prayed, 'Lord help the missionaries to understand us and help us to understand the missionaries.' But we worked well with them because we loved them. When you really love someone, you don't see the differences, you just see the similarities."

I am taken aback. "When you really love someone, you don't see the differences, you just see the similarities." This profound thought is stated with little emphasis, wisdom from the heart. A gem of gold to be shared with others.

It was evident that their people also loved the missionary family when one church member exclaimed, "You know, you just pure seem like kinfolk!" And they were kin—through the bloodline of Christ.

As we chat, Leola's trademark, a pleasant smile, never leaves her face. Seated on a dark blue sofa in her warm and attractive home, she chats about the diverse responsibilities the couple faced when they accepted the assignment. "Before the former missionary couple retired, I asked the Isaacses, 'My, how do you hold up?' They told me that the Lord would give me extra strength when I needed it. And He did.

"I relied heavily on a favorite Scripture from Philippians, the fourth chapter and thirteenth verse, 'I can do all things through Christ which strengtheneth me.' We began to work with the churches by teaching study courses and encouraging the people to strengthen their Sunday Schools. Each summer I worked in Vacation Bible School in nine or ten churches, taught homemaker groups, bought groceries, and cooked for two week-long camps— one for boys and another week for the girls. Elbert became a 'Jack-of-all-trades,' from preaching and pastoring to plumbing and electrical work.

"I thought I should have all the answers and then I realized I could learn from the people," Leola reflects, as if lost momentarily in her own remembrances. "A group of the ladies wanted to plan an event, a ladies-only meeting. I immediately thought, this will not work. There are too many children to care for. The ladies, undaunted, assured me they could leave the children for a night with family members or friends. The year was 1976. As plans progressed someone suggested that everyone dress to commemorate the two-hundredth birthday of our country. Again, I fretted and questioned. I thought some might not participate if they were unable to have a long dress for this occasion.

"Now I recall that night as very special. Each woman found child care and arrived in a long dress. An unmarried lady, Miss Lois Privett, from the state mission office, captivated the women with her challenge. It was a wonderful night. I had listened to the people. I began to understand that God never expected me to have all the answers."

Perhaps God was preparing Leola for other more important questions on life's horizon. The very heart of Christian missions is allowing others to see in our lives a change made possible by God's unselfish love. Leola demonstrated her love in a dramatic way in 1987 when she donated a kidney to her older son, Glenn. However, the years to come would bring some questions that seem to have no ready answer. Leola tells the story.

"My son Joe and his twelve-year-old son, Joey, jumped into the Gulf water for a morning swim. Not far from shore the father called out to his son, 'Joey I am dying.' The son struggled to help his father but was too small for the task. His only choice was to leave his father and swim back to shore for help." The physician ministered to the family as he explained that even a doctor could not have made a difference if one had been present. Joe died from a massive heart attack at age thirty-eight. Just two years later Leola lost her lifelong mate and father of her three children.

Perhaps God was preparing Leola for other more important questions on life's horizon. The very heart of Christian missions is allowing others to see in our lives a change made possible by God's unselfish love.

Despite unanswered questions, Leola continues in retirement years to be active in her local church. In addition to teaching an adult Sunday School class and singing in the church choir, she serves as Women's Missionary Union Director at Memorial Baptist Church in Citronelle, Alabama. Under her leadership, the church is involved in mission outreach in many areas including a ministry to seamen who arrive in the nearby port city of Mobile, and a ministry to the local children's home. And God continues to bless the couple's longtime mission endeavor with the Mowa tribe.

The evangelistic messages, proclaimed through the years at Family Camp, reached many for Christ. Individuals answered calls into the ministry. Commitments were made during those services that are evidenced today in the lives of those who made them. Many faithfully follow in His footsteps and look forward to His return, a time for singing the final verse of the hymn, "How Great Thou Art."

When Christ shall come with shout of acclamation,
And take me home, what joy shall fill my heart!
Then I shall bow in humble adoration
And there proclaim, my God, how great Thou art!

Leola's Favorite Hymn

HE HIDETH MY SOUL

Fannie J. Crosby

A wonderful Saviour is Jesus my Lord,
A wonderful Saviour to me,
He hideth my soul in the cleft of the rock,
Where rivers of pleasure I see.

A wonderful Saviour is Jesus my Lord,
He taketh my burden away,
He holdeth me up, and I shall not be moved,
He giveth me strength as my day.

With numberless blessings each moment He crowns,
And filled with His fullness divine,
I sing in my rapture, Oh, glory to God
For such a Redeemer as mine!

When clothed in His brightness, transported I rise
To meet Him in clouds of the sky,
His perfect salvation, His wonderful love,
I'll shout with the millions on high.

Chorus:

He hideth my soul in the cleft of the rock
That shadows a dry, thirsty land;
He hideth my life in the depths of His love,
And covers me there with His hand,
And covers me there with His hand.

Leola's Favorite Poem

WHEN I MEET THE MASTER FACE TO FACE

I had walked life's way with an easy tread,
Had followed where pleasure and comfort led,
Until one day in a quiet place
I met the Master face to face.

With station and rank and wealth for my goal,
Much thought for my body and none for my soul,
I had entered to win in life's mad race
When I met my Master face to face.

I met Him and knew Him and blushed to see
That His eyes full of sorrow were fixed on me;
And I faltered and fell at His feet that day,
While my castles melted and vanished away.

Melted and vanished and in their place
Naught else did I see but the Master's face,
And I cried aloud, "Oh make me meek
To follow the steps of Thy wounded feet."
My thoughts are now for the souls of men,
I have lost my life to find it again,
E're since one day in a quiet place
I met my Master face to face.

—Selected

A Recipe From the Mowa Tribe

SWEET POTATO PONE

6-8 small sweet potatoes, grated

2 cups sugar

1/4 cup white corn syrup

1 tablespoon cinnamon

1 teaspoon nutmeg

pinch of salt

1/2 cup margarine

2 tablespoons flour

1 teaspoon vanilla flavoring

10-12 ounces water

*Mix together and bake in a rectangular pan
at 350 degrees for 2 hours.*

*NOTE FROM LEOLA: This recipe, supplied by Lucille Weaver, is a
favorite of mine.*

Elaine
A Portrait of Compassion

"Be kind and compassionate to one another,
forgiving each other, just as in Christ God forgave you."

(Ephesians 4:32)

I watch carefully for white paint on the curb, my landmark for turning once again into the driveway. Trees and dense foliage totally obscure the restored seventy-year-old home from heavily traveled Cottage Hill Road. A winding pavement directs me past flowering beds of spring plants to Elaine's front door. Born to my mother's sister Naomi and her husband Charlie, Elaine, the firstborn child of my generation, is teasingly called the "oldest cousin." She greets me at the door and welcomes me into a home that I love to enter.

Born in November 1926, in West Palm Beach, Florida, Elaine has often heard the story of how her parents fled with their baby to a hotel for shelter as a powerful gulf storm approached land. When they were all safely inside the hotel, Charlie and the other men used slats from hotel beds to secure mattresses over windows in an effort to protect their families. Their lives were spared but the hurricane devastated the city and left the family with few possessions. They traveled north to Mobile, Alabama, lived briefly in Montgomery, then moved to Atlanta, Georgia, where they attended Kirkwood Baptist Church.

"I was not planning on being a good child," Elaine said. "I was a cowboy-and-Indian kid. I wore a holster and carried guns. One day the pastor, Rev. White, came to our home to visit. It was then—I was nine years old—when I made my profession of faith. Since joining the church, and being baptized at that young age, I have always been in church. Much later, at one point in time, I realized I was not really worshiping. I had lost confidence in church people. I saw no compassion. There were other times when I struggled." Her voice trails off to a whisper as her eyes reveal the pain she felt.

We sit silently. I am family. I know a part of Elaine's story. *I think about how deeply we can wound others when we, who name the name of Christ, fail to follow His example.*

I was jarred back to the present when Elaine asked, "Do we want to have our tea here or shall we move to the kitchen?" A room with a view, Elaine's kitchen is a perfect place for tea and hot blueberry muffins served on delicate Bavarian china. Bill, Elaine's husband of fifty-five years, comes in from working outside, looking for something cold to drink. We kid a moment about Elaine's pretty napkins matching the china, her personal way of providing homemade hospitality.

Afternoon sunshine seeps sheepishly through the heavy outside foliage as we settle again in the comfort of her living room. Elaine continues, "We moved from Atlanta back to West Palm Beach and finally settled in Mobile when I was in high school.

"*I* was not planning on being a good child," Elaine said. "I was a cowboy-and-Indian kid. I wore a holster and carried guns. One day the pastor, Rev. White, came to our home to visit. It was then—I was nine years old—when I made my profession of faith.

"Bill came home to Mobile in January 1946 after he was discharged from the navy. We dated until he left for summer school at Carson Newman College. That same year we married on August 18, honeymooned for a few days in Gatlinburg, Tennessee, then on to school for fall semester. It was a 'have-to' marriage," Elaine teases. "Bill had to have someone to help him pass his college English courses." The couple worked and attended school with Bill graduating before they returned to Mobile, where he began a long career in real estate.

Elaine continued her undergraduate studies and taught in Sunday School, sang in her church choir, and also in a church ladies' ensemble. Three women in the choir became steadfast friends: Elaine, Betty, and Becky. The three sang together for twenty years. They ate together weekly after choir practice. "Betty was a most unusual person," Elaine volunteers. "Each afternoon after work she dropped by to see someone who was lonely, who might have a specific need, or who just needed to see a friendly face. She always took a small gift, a handkerchief, a flower from her yard, or, perhaps, a book."

Betty, who never married and who had few living relatives,

was confronted with every woman's fear—cancer. "She never fully recovered following that initial surgery." Pain crept across Elaine's face as she continued.

"She battled cancer for two years. Betty had been a Sunday School department director for years, giving her time and energy to the church, yet those in the church did little. I even called one woman in the church and asked her to stay with Betty or at least come to visit. I learned that some people who wouldn't dream of missing a church meeting would not lift a finger to meet the needs of another person." Elaine postponed graduate studies to spend time daily with her friend.

During the two years that Betty battled for her life, Elaine was at her side. "I went to her home almost every day. We had some good times together. When she felt like going, I would take her out for a ride. We might take a picnic lunch to the park or ride across the bay if the dogwoods were blooming.

"The last three months she was in the hospital I fought with the nurses every night trying to get her some help, trying to get enough pain medication to make her comfortable."

Telling Betty's story evokes some of the pain Elaine must have felt during those long months. But Elaine's compassion quickly becomes more evident than the pain.

"You spent every night at the hospital those three months?" I ask.

I realize I was wrong to think I already knew this story. I am amazed. How could anyone do this? What a display of compassion for a friend in need!

"I stayed every night except Saturdays from Easter Sunday until the end of June, when she died. Bill made it possible for me to be there," Elaine says. We joke for a moment about the girls in our family marrying good men. "I couldn't have done it without Bill's support," Elaine says. "He helped with the children, everything. I left every night at eight-thirty and returned the next morning in time to get the children off to school. I slept during the morning, cooked our evening meal, then returned to the hospital."

After Betty's death Elaine returned to school to earn a master's degree in education, plans she had postponed when she became the caregiver for her friend. And she began her own ministry. "My reaction was to fill Betty's place in meeting the needs of lonely and hurting people," Elaine said. "I began visiting a friend's mother who was ill, and another friend's father in a nursing home. I had six or so people that I visited once a month. As those people died, I did not take on new people to visit, because I needed to give more attention to Mother."

The respect I have always had for Elaine is replaced that afternoon with awe.

She quickly turns the attention from herself to her present Sunday School class.

"The class I am in today is the best at taking care of each other that I have seen," Elaine says. "There is a real need within churches for people to minister. I know everyone cannot do this but there is such a need for compassion. Compassion may be the most important thing we have to offer to others."

I listen intently and repeat in my mind, Compassion may be the most important thing we have to offer to others. Compassion—taking a stand with others in distress. Is this not a composite of the life of Christ?

Elaine knows what those with hurt in their lives need most. Five years to the day after Betty's surgery, another Easter Sunday,

Elaine entered the hospital for a radical mastectomy. "It never occurred to me that I would not survive," she said. She has been cancer-free since that surgery in 1973.

Three years ago, while caring for her own ninety-five-year-old mother, Elaine suffered a heart attack and a stroke during the surgery that followed. The stroke left her vision seriously impaired. I commented on her survival and the determination she displayed during recovery. "I was thankful when I was spared from cancer," she said "When I had the heart attack and stroke, it did occur to me that I might not survive. However, since I have survived three of the most dreaded illnesses known, I believe God has something for me to do, and I hope I am doing it."

On most trips, after much insistence from the other sisters, Naomi demonstrated her flapper walk from the 1920s. This behavior, often forbidden to the sisters in their youth, became hysterical after-dinner entertainment when they reached eighty years of age.

I look at my watch and realize that we have spent almost two hours together without touching on Elaine's ministry closest to my heart—her family ministry. "Oh, we had fun!" Elaine exclaimed. I knew they did. I had a day-by-day report after each trip. Elaine took her mother, Aunt Naomi, and Aunt Tot, as well as my mother, on driving trips. "Once a year we took a long trip— to the Smoky Mountains; Knoxville, Tennessee; North Carolina; Atlanta, Georgia; or Nashville, Tennessee to visit the Grand Old Opry. We must have made five or six trips to Disney World, Epcot, Cypress Gardens and Silver Springs. In the middle of the day we had a hot meal and at night we had a picnic in the room. They had a good time."

As I recall from Mama's account, they had more than a picnic in the room at night—they had live entertainment. On most trips, after much insistence from the other sisters, Naomi demonstrated her flapper walk from the 1920s. This behavior, often forbidden to the sisters in their youth, became hysterical after-dinner entertainment when they reached eighty years of age.

But as the sisters climbed beyond their eightieth birthdays, they didn't feel as comfortable on long trips. They wanted to stay closer to home. It was then that Elaine took the group to her beach house for two-night stays several times each year.

Those trips were important to my mother and her sisters. I appreciated the one who was willing to be organizer, driver, chaperone, tour director, and caretaker for four. It takes a special person to entertain seniors—a compassionate person.

Elaine continues, almost as if she is thinking aloud. "I overheard a nursing home resident say once that one mother can raise five or six children but those five or six children cannot take care of one mother. I think that is one of the saddest things I have ever heard. Christian people need to be more caring. We need to pattern daily the compassionate attitude of Jesus. He didn't force others to do anything. Rather, He displayed virtues for them to see. And we should be doing the same."

For Elaine and Bill, displaying the attitude of Christ involves an international adventure. Elaine tells the story.

"I had gone to France on a Sister City tour in the spring of 1975. When I arrived home and stepped off the plane, Bill greeted me by asking if I would like to sponsor a Vietnamese family. Saigon had fallen to the North Vietnamese, and refugees in the South had escaped with the aid of Americans to the islands of the South

Pacific or to the United States. I can tell you that the thought had never crossed my mind, but I agreed to look into sponsoring a family.

"Bill purchased a two-story house and for weeks, with the help of family and friends, we cleaned and furnished the house. One day Bill's mother was cleaning the kitchen and trying to get the grease off the stove. Finally she decided it looked impossible, so she just stopped and prayed that someone would donate a stove. It happened before the cock crowed twice! Someone called and said they had a stove to donate. Bill and George, a friend who owned a truck, picked up the stove and gathered other donations of furniture, dishes, and appliances.

"Bill found two families with four children each. The brothers had been separated from their parents and did not want to leave Eglin Air Force Base without locating them. Bill promised to locate the parents through the Red Cross. (They were located and the family was reunited in Mobile.) The two brothers and their families came back to Mobile with us that day to the house on Chamberlain Avenue where one family lived downstairs and the other, upstairs. They literally came with the clothes on their backs. We took the children for immunizations, registered them for school, and shopped for clothes with money generous friends donated.

"Only one of the brothers spoke a little English, but they were fast learners. Soon these children, who had arrived in Mobile not understanding or speaking a word of English, were at the top of their classes. The families prospered and became American citizens of whom we are proud. They all have college degrees and good jobs. Most have married and have children of their own."

For days after our meeting I would contemplate Elaine's story—a twentieth-century Good Samaritan parable. Her words, "We need to pattern the compassionate attitude of Jesus," took on new meaning. Rather than a man injured beside a lonely road, Elaine's story focused on three generations of a family stranded in a foreign country in need of kindness.

When we spoke, Elaine repeated her comment, "I believe that God has more for me to do." After pausing momentarily, she added, "I just hope that I am doing it."

I know that she is doing what God has for her to do. Every opportunity that does not require driving is an opportunity Elaine welcomes as one to reach out to others. She accompanies a friend as they minister to a Sunday School classmate over lunch. Her e-mail and telephone calls offer encouraging words. She continues to host a New Year's Day celebration for family and friends. The older generation gathers to play table games for an afternoon at her house. Elaine can't take food to a home where there is illness, but she can bake a wonderful lemon cake for Bill to deliver. I know. One arrived at my home.

And she has a bountiful supply of compassionate wisdom waiting to be shared.

If I can stop one heart from breaking,

I shall not live in vain;

If I can ease one life the aching,

Or cool one pain,

Or help one fainting robin

Unto his nest again,

I shall not live in vain.

Emily Dickinson

Elaine's Favorite Hymn

ONCE FOR ALL

Phillip P. Bliss

Free from the law, oh, happy condition!
Jesus hath bled, and there is remission;
Cursed by the law and bruised by the fall,
Grace hath redeemed us once for all.

Now we are free—there's no condemnation;
Jesus provides a perfect salvation;
"Come unto Me," oh, hear His sweet call,
Come, and He saves us once for all.

Children of God—oh, glorious calling,
Surely His grace will keep us from falling;
Pressing from death to life at His call,
Blessed salvation once for all.

Once for all—oh, sinner, receive it;
Once for all—oh, doubter, believe it;
Cling to the cross, the burden will fall,
Christ hath redeemed us once for all.

A Recipe From Elaine's Kitchen

SPINACH MADELEINE

2 packages frozen chopped spinach

4 tablespoons butter

2 tablespoons flour

2 tablespoons onion, chopped

1/2 cup evaporated milk

1/2 cup vegetable broth

1/2 teaspoon black pepper

3/4 teaspoon celery salt

3/4 teaspoon garlic salt

Salt to taste

6 oz. roll of jalapeno cheese

1 tablespoon Worcestershire sauce

Cook spinach according to directions on the package. Drain well and reserve broth (water in which spinach was cooked). Melt butter in saucepan over low heat. Add flour, stirring until blended and smooth but not brown. Add liquid slowly, stirring constantly to avoid lumps. Cook until smooth and thick; continue stirring. Add seasonings and cheese, which has been cut into small pieces. Stir until melted. Combine with cooked spinach. This may be served immediately or put into a casserole and topped with buttered bread crumbs. The flavor is improved if the latter is done and kept in refrigerator overnight. This may also be frozen. Serves five or six.

NOTE FROM ELAINE: So different!

Helen
A Portrait of Perseverance

"Consider it pure joy, my brothers, whenever you face trials of
many kinds, because you know that the testing of your faith
develops perseverance. Perseverance must finish its work so that
you may be mature and complete, not lacking anything."

(James 1:2-4)

Today I enjoy lunch with Helen in the dining hall of
lovely Westminster Village. The calm nature and tranquil spirit
that drew me to Helen when we met more than twenty years ago
remains today. As we fill our trays with sliced turkey, dressing with
gravy, vegetables, and dessert from the buffet, Helen pauses often,
offering encouraging words to each person she meets.

After finishing lunch we walk though a hallway to the
comfortable second-story, two-bedroom apartment Helen shares
with her husband. It is a balmy spring day, and Helen suggests

that we visit on the outside balcony. Overlooking a courtyard filled with multicolored spring blossoms and surrounded by sounds of nature, Helen reverently shares their story.

"John preached on Sunday at Clark Air Force Base in the Philippines. The Scripture was from Psalm 92 and the sermon title was 'Being Secure in an Insecure World.' The next afternoon we experienced that sermon as we headed for Baguio accompanied by another couple, Bob and Jan Nash. On a steep mountain road John sensed what he first thought was a problem with the car. He pulled off the road and momentarily, a huge boulder crashed on the road beside us. Then everything seemed to break loose. We felt three motions: waves, zigzags, and sudden drops. The loudest thunder we had ever heard came from inside the earth as boulders and debris tumbled down the mountainside.

"A woman ran toward us screaming, 'My baby, my baby.' Her young child and a niece were playing in a nearby stream when an avalanche covered them. Relatives who lived nearby pulled them from the rubble. One child was dead, the other, alive, but unconscious," Helen relates softly. "I was realistic. I remember thinking, *Well, this is it.* I was scared. But I had peace." On a 15-

month mission assignment in 1990, the retired couple was experiencing an earthquake that devastated parts of the island of Luzon and measured 7.8 in magnitude.

Born in the small town of Louisville, Alabama, Helen was the only child of Harrison and Jennie Hurst Williamson. "I did not come from a strong Christian home but I always had a leaning toward the Lord," Helen begins. "I made an early profession of faith in my heart, then made that decision public and was baptized when I was twelve. When I was about fourteen years old, I made a deeper commitment to Christ during a revival at the local Methodist church. Some in the family might have thought I was a bit fanatical."

The small town school she attended may not have been the best, but it was there that Helen learned to study. She felt she had a responsibility to excel because she was the only child of her family. Her dedication to learning paid dividends when she received a scholarship and attended Huntington College in Montgomery, Alabama.

In 1943, as a first-year college student, Helen was invited to a roof garden party at First Baptist Church, in Montgomery. That night Helen met a young man named John who was a member of the church. "I did not like him. I thought he was a show-off, conceited, and stuck-up," she said.

During World War II John was sent overseas, serving as an officer in the Corp. of Engineers. Helen transferred later to Auburn University. "The Auburn days were among the happiest days of my life," Helen reminisces. "It was a time of maturing for me, mentally and spiritually. During the summer before my senior year I was one of a committee of four chosen to select the new Baptist Student Union president." The other committee members knew that John was returning from service to complete his degree. They wanted to elect him president of the Baptist Student Union but Helen, recalling her earlier impression, did not vote for John. The other three members outvoted her and John was elected president.

Helen quickly realized that John was very different from the young man she had met years earlier at the roof garden party. After experiencing the horrors and devastation of war, he had changed from a frivolous boy to a mature man. John felt called to Christian service, and he redirected his college courses toward an undergraduate liberal arts degree to qualify him for seminary acceptance.

Following night committee meetings, John escorted Helen across the Auburn campus to the home where she lived. Romance blossomed. Helen had reservations about their relationship. While overseas John had received a "Dear John" letter from his sweetheart, and Helen wondered if he might be on the rebound. She also knew John's heart was in Japan. Helen thought he might want to return as a missionary, something she might not be able to do as an only child.

John did make a decision to go to Japan, but love prevailed. Helen and John married in August 1947 and immediately moved to Fort Worth, Texas, where John enrolled in Southwestern Baptist Theological Seminary. Helen, from rural Alabama, recalls thinking when they finally arrived in Fort Worth that they had already moved halfway around the world!

The move was an act of faith. Even though Helen had a degree, there were no job openings in her field. They had to survive six months before John started drawing 94 dollars per month under the G.I. Bill, money made available to veterans to further their education. "I worked in various stores and in the seminary library," Helen says. "It was our time in life to learn about perseverance, to learn that if we depended on the Lord, He would provide. We had to depend on the Lord. We did our part and God provided.

"I had always felt my calling was to be a Christian mother. I was immature compared to others around me. I prayed, 'Lord, give me some opportunities to grow.' The seminary president and his wife had a handicapped child, and they were looking for a couple to live in their garage apartment and help with the child. Going to live there and enjoying their fellowship was a learning experience. We had opportunity to observe their Christian maturity. They became our surrogate parents, our counselors."

> "*I* knew that I would have a child. One of the greatest times for me spiritually was this assurance from the Lord. I recall singing and meditating on the words of the hymn 'Have Faith in God.'"

The summer after John completed his first year of seminary the couple faced their first personal heartache. Helen lost the baby she was carrying. "When a second miscarriage followed," Helen continues, "I began to understand that we learn some things only through sorrow. This was the time when I grew up spiritually. Our faith was deepened, and we experienced closeness with God. I still believed that God was going to give us children."

"We learn some things only through sorrow." A statement filled with wisdom from one who knows and is willing to share golden wisdom with today's woman.

The couple found a Christian doctor to work with them. Treatment was expensive.

At seven months Helen delivered a three-pound baby boy who lived four days—another abrupt ending to a wonderful anticipation. "We had no money," Helen says. "The seminary faculty and our fellow students from Auburn contributed, almost to the penny, the amount needed to pay the hospital bill and burial expenses for the baby."

Tears spilled from Helen's eyes. I offer, "I am sorry this is so hard for you."

Helen quietly answers. "No, it is therapeutic."

I reflect on the Scripture Helen mentioned earlier, " . . . knowing that tribulation produces perseverance . . ." I realize that the qualities I admire so much in Helen were birthed in tribulation. There are no arms so empty as those of a mother with no baby to hold.

Meanwhile the couple's commitment to missions remained strong. Seminary graduation was a time of separating from parents and friends. John and Helen were committed to Japan. But the Foreign Mission Board felt Japan, at that time, did not have adequate facilities for a high-risk pregnancy and delivery. They advised the couple to have their first baby in the States, so John returned to seminary to work on a doctorate.

"I knew that I would have a child. One of the greatest times for me spiritually was this assurance from the Lord. I recall singing and meditating on the words of the hymn 'Have Faith in God.'"

Another pregnancy, and in the fifth month the routine doctor visit rendered distressing news. Well-meaning friends told the couple they should just accept the fact that they were not going to have a child and apply to adopt. John and Helen prayed and their prayers were answered, as God revealed to Helen through prayer and meditation that she needed to just trust Him.

"This was another time of growth for you?" I ask.

"Yes, I was learning that children are truly a gift from the Lord, a miracle of the Lord."

At Helen's next visit the doctor said, "I don't know what has happened but the lab levels have changed." And when that same doctor delivered the baby (who was named Paul), he said, "The Lord didn't just give you a baby. He gave you a nine-pound, five-ounce whopper!"

John continued to work on his doctorate and taught at a local college. The couple was enjoying their son, Paul, and as a family of three, they were active in their church. John and Helen applied again to the Foreign Mission Board for appointment, only to be turned down because of a medical problem detected during their screenings.

In a sense they did go to a mission field, a home mission field. A small group of Christians, meeting in a house in Dothan, Alabama, called John to be pastor of what would become Calvary Baptist Church. By now they were a family of four: John, Helen, Paul, and a baby girl, Janet.

John left the family in Dothan for six weeks to finish his

dissertation. After he left, Helen realized she was expecting another child. She was sick and had two babies to care for, yet she decided to wait until John returned home to tell him so he would not be distracted from his work. After a long drive from Fort Worth to southeastern Alabama, John arrived home one morning at four A.M. As he cuddled baby Janet in his arms, John said, "Oh, she is so sweet!"

"Wouldn't you like to have another one?" Helen asked. Not many months later Beth arrived to complete the family. "The years in Dothan at Calvary Baptist Church were good years," Helen recalls.

The Thomas family marriage was a saga of beginnings. John was instrumental in establishing Calvary Baptist Church in Dothan, then he served First Baptist Church in Troy, Alabama. It was while serving there that the couple received a telephone call from the president of the newly chartered Mobile College. That call propelled the family toward Mobile, Alabama.

For the first time they began to understand why their life's plan included a doctorate for John. This move, from pastoring to college professor, was a step of faith. On paper, it seemed financially impossible to make the move. But the couple, accustomed to unexpected turns in the road, headed to Mobile. Helen applied for a job teaching in public school. It was her first time to teach—sixteen years after graduating from college. "The Lord enables you to do what you need to do," Helen says. "I know He does!"

John finished his career teaching at the University of Mobile (formerly known as Mobile College). The couple watched as many of John's students volunteered for the mission field. Helen retired from the school system after working as a counselor with troubled youth.

Even retirement resulted in new beginnings. Seeing firsthand the needs of today's troubled youth, the couple was involved in helping to establish Baldwin Youth Services, an intervention program under the auspices of the court. Helen and John worked with those who envisioned a new church in their area. They were instrumental in the birth and growth of that church, Eastern Shore Baptist Church, and today are faithful members there.

Yet life's work was not over for this couple. One might consider that Helen and John's lifelong lessons of perseverance, experience, and hope were the university classes of life that God used to prepare them, missionaries at heart, for their work in the Philippines following retirement. "We spent that first night after the earthquake stranded on the road between Clark Field and Baguio with devastation encircling us. Not knowing what we should do, the next morning we put some things in a bag, left the car, and started walking toward Baguio. We found we could not walk in that direction—there was no road or path to walk on. We returned

Yet life's work was not over for this couple. One might consider that Helen and John's lifelong lessons of perseverance, experience, and hope were the university classes of life that God used to prepare them, missionaries at heart, for their work in the Philippines following retirement.

to the car and prayed for wisdom to know what to do. Later we walked south. The rock slides ceased for awhile and we walked and crawled over huge rocks. After walking south for a distance we found a flat area and a busload of people, also stranded.

"The Filipino people were hospitable. The bus driver gave us permission to sleep on the bus. John and Bob went to nearby huts and bought rice. A rice and sardine mixture, with fresh vegetables added from a stranded truck, was cooked over an open fire in a borrowed wash pot. The first day banana leaves were used as plates, fingers as utensils, and space behind an open umbrella, a restroom.

"Mountain residents attempting to walk out carried handwritten messages that missionaries were stranded. We wanted our families and colleagues to know that we were alive, but stranded. We were never sure," Helen says, "that the notes made it to their destination until we heard on the bus radio report that a message had reached authorities that American missionaries were stranded. They warned us that we should not to try to walk out.

"The second night we had a terrible tremor. It shook the bus like it was a toy. The bus was crowded with people lying on the floor. A native lawyer spoke urgently, 'I know there are Christians on this bus and we need to pray.' Prayers were voiced in many languages and dialects. Then a young girl spontaneously started singing:

'We are one in the bond of love,

We are one in the bond of love,

We have joined our spirits with the spirit of God,

We are one in the bond of love.'

Although the world was falling apart around us, this small incident united Christians on that bus in something greater than this world. It was a glimpse of heaven.

"United States helicopters flew over, and one Navy helicopter dropped K rations but there was no place to land. The men located a nearby school with a basketball field and a space was cleared for landing. On Thursday, the fourth day, Filipino helicopters landed, bringing doctors. They treated the sick and carried the seriously injured to safety. Among the first to be carried out was the child found unconscious on Monday."

Later a small helicopter, resembling a mosquito and used for transporting Wycliff translators to inaccessible areas, landed nearby. The pilot announced that they were looking for American missionaries. The group of four, John and Helen, Bob and Jan, replied, "You have found them!"

During the days following their rescue, Helen was asked to tell her experiences many times. "I realized it would be easy to have a prideful attitude, to think—look how strong I was to have survived such an experience. But I learned otherwise. As the strong aftershocks continued, I experienced great fear. I was reminded that it was only through God's grace, not my strength, that I could endure. God even used my weakness. Because of it I was able to relate to wives of international students who were also traumatized by the violent quakes. A bond was formed as we dealt with our fears and encouraged each other."

It has been ten years since the couple returned to the United States after finishing their mission assignment. John's health has failed, and he is in constant pain. Helen reflects, "Since I have been a caregiver, I have observed others who unselfishly give of themselves without applause. There is no high drama in their lives, just monotonous mundane sameness, yet they are faithful. Perhaps by God's standards these saints measure higher than survivors of high drama."

Today Helen continues to serve in her own quiet way as she worships at Eastern Shore Baptist Church and serves as an encourager to family and friends. Helen's demeanor is tranquil; her life radiates calmness, and her face is a portrait of perseverance.

Helen's Favorite Hymn

HAVE FAITH IN GOD

B. B. McKinney

Have faith in God when your pathway is lonely,
He sees and knows all the way you have trod;
Never alone are the least of His children;
Have faith in God, have faith in God.

Have faith in God when your prayers are unanswered,
Your earnest plea He will never forget;
Wait on the Lord, trust His word and be patient,
Have faith in God, He'll answer yet.

Have faith in God in your pain and your sorrow,
His heart is touched with your grief and despair;
Cast all your care and your burdens upon Him,
And leave them there, oh, leave them there.

Have faith in God though all else fail about you;
Have faith in God, He provides for His own;
He cannot fail though all kingdoms shall perish,
He rules, He reigns upon His throne.

Have faith in God, He's on His throne;
Have faith in God, He watches o'er His own;
He cannot fail, He must prevail:
Have faith in God, have faith in God.

A Recipe From Helen's Kitchen

SQUASH DELIGHT

1 pound yellow squash, cooked

1/2 stick butter or margarine

1 tablespoon sugar

1/2 cup mayonnaise

1/2 cup onion, chopped

1/2 cup pimento, chopped

1/2 cup green pepper, chopped

1-2 eggs, beaten

1 cup grated cheese

Sauté onion and green peppers in butter. Drain squash. Add onion, green pepper, and pimento. Blend until you cannot tell it is squash. To the squash mixture add sugar, eggs (beaten), mayonnaise, salt, pepper, and cheese. Mix together. Pour into casserole and top with crushed Ritz crackers. Dot with butter. Bake at 350 degrees for 35-40 minutes, or until mixture is firm but not dry.

Ellen
A Portrait of Serenity

"Cast thy burden upon the LORD, and he shall sustain thee:
he shall never suffer the righteous to be moved."

(Psalm 55:22, KJV)

O pening a copy of *Daily Strength for Daily Needs* Ellen turns
to page seventy-one and reads aloud to me the words of H.
W. Smith:

"The circumstances of her life she could not alter, but
she took them to the Lord, and handed them over to His
management; and then she believed that He took it, and
she left all the responsibility and the worry and the anxiety
with Him. As often as the anxieties returned she gave
them back; and the result was that, although the
circumstances remained unchanged, her soul was kept in

perfect peace in the midst of them."

The small leather-bound brown book, given by Ellen's father-in-law to his wife in 1942, is one that Ellen cherishes. The wisdom in this writing by Mr. Smith depicts the lifestyle she strives to live daily. "Even though the circumstances of life often cannot be changed, I can hand them over to Him and have peace," Ellen says.

Six years ago on a Swiss Air jet midway between Istanbul, Turkey, and Frankfurt, Germany, I was an eyewitness to Ellen's calmness and tranquillity. The morning flight had required leaving our hotel early in preparation for the return trip to the United States. Finally airborne, I settled in with a pillow and a book—the perfect air prescription for an instant nap. Momentarily, Margery, our tour director, awakened me with a light tap on the shoulder. "J. T. is having difficulty breathing. Please come check on him."

I quickly located Ellen's husband, J. T., seated in an aisle seat. He was anxious, laboring to breathe, and sweating profusely (all symptoms of a heart attack). However, his pulse was strong and his heart rhythm regular. Flight attendants provided oxygen and alerted the pilot of the emergency. Two attendants and I, all trained in CPR, quietly planned our roles if cardiac arrest occurred in the air. Although I felt uncomfortable and wondered how close we were to an airport that could accommodate the large plane, I assured J. T. that his heart sounded strong and regular and he was going to be just fine. Throughout the hour-long experience 35,000 feet in the air, Ellen constantly reassured her mate while remaining outwardly calm and serene. Paramedics met the plane in Frankfurt. A physician evaluated and treated J. T. and the couple returned to the United States later that day.

Today I drive down a narrow thoroughfare that lazily curves its way through the Spring Hill area of Mobile, Alabama, to the home of Ellen and J. T. Arendall. The beautiful Charleston-style brick home offers a glimpse of the past. I am reminded of a time when life was tranquil, people sat in parlors and chatted for hours, and older women shared golden wisdom as they mentored younger generations. Today Ellen, relaxed and composed, shares secrets from her lifetime of Christian commitment.

Ellen made her debut in the world just past midnight on

November 14, 1917. She describes her early years as very happy times. Her father was co-owner of Kitrell Milling, an early Dodge Motor Company dealership in Mobile. With this and other business ventures he provided well for his family and invested wisely for the future. When her mother had to live away from home for fifteen months to be treated for tuberculosis, an aunt and uncle moved into their home to help with the three children. But it was her father who saw that their shoes were polished on Saturday night and offering envelopes prepared for Sunday School on Sunday morning.

At the tender age of eight, Ellen sat beside their family friend—her minister—on a pew in the old Dauphin Way Baptist Church and gave her heart to Christ. The man who led her through this decision to accept Christ, Dr. Charles B. Arendall, would later become her father-in-law.

"I met J. T. when I was six years old," Ellen proudly declares. "And we were dating when we were fourteen. We had been spending time together at church socials for more than a year. Our families were close friends so we were just always together. We went to church or other group activities on Friday night, but on Saturday we had a date, usually a movie at the Saenger Theater in downtown Mobile. It cost forty cents to sit downstairs but only twenty-five cents for the balcony. So we sat in the balcony.

"J. T. borrowed his father's car which had a rumble seat. He got his older friend to drive us so we could sit in the rumble seat together. He was my best friend," Ellen speaks with a twinkle in her eyes, "and he still is today."

Life took a sharp turn for Ellen during that fourteenth year. Her father died. "I knew my Daddy loved me and in those fourteen years he imparted some wisdom to me that I continue to value today." Ellen speaks in a hushed voice. I asked what wisdom she captured from her father. She answers simply, "Family is important and the Sabbath should be observed as a holy day." This wisdom, given by a father to his young daughter, continues to shape Ellen's life. Each Lord's Day she regards as holy, and family remains important.

"Dr. Arendall became a father figure after my father died, so J.T. and I grew up like family." Ellen continues speaking, her smiling countenance belying the difficult emotional time following the death of her father. "I attended a girl's preparatory school in Mobile then left for Judson College. My father had been a trustee there, and I always wanted to be a 'Judson Girl.' J. T. was in school in Virginia at the University of Richmond. We both spent time socializing with others during those four years of college when we were separated. I guess you could say we dated others. But everyone knew that we belonged to each other and that someday we would marry."

And they did marry—after each graduated from college. "Mother and I spent the year after I graduated planning the wedding and just being together," Ellen recalls. " J. T. was working at a bank and the bank policy was that employees could not marry until they were making one-hundred dollars a month. J. T. was only making forty-nine dollars per month. So he quit his job and began working at a furniture store, with no guarantee of pay, but free to marry. J. T. gave me a diamond engagement ring on January 16, 1939, the seventh anniversary of our first date. And we married in June of that year." Today Ellen wears that same ring that J. T. gave to her more than sixty-two years ago.

Committed to their own marriage, and faithful to Christ in their church, the couple, along with friends, Win and Nell

Ritchie, felt led to begin a Sunday School class for young married couples. This was a first for their church, Dauphin Way Baptist. Reaching out to young couples within the church as well as to newcomers to Mobile, they touched many for Christ. But it was in the early 1960s that the visionary couple, now members of Spring Hill Baptist Church, saw the need to touch another group—singles—within and outside the church. They began as a couple to reach out to those who were lonely, single again, and hurting, and others who were church members but not attending regularly.

Perhaps Ellen was drawing from her experience during summers spent at Ridgecrest Baptist Assembly in North Carolina. "One of my favorite preachers, Dr. S. D. Gordon, was also an author of many books. My favorite of his was *Quiet Talks on Prayer*. My mother and I went to conferences and worship services every day. Dr. Gordon was a unique preacher. He would stop in the middle of a sermon and ask, 'Are you listening? Are you listening with the ears of your heart?'" It was in those services that Ellen learned to listen with the ears of her heart, and many years later found herself seeing and responding to an unmet need.

Outreach ministries are often an outgrowth of a personal need. But J. T. and Ellen reached out to singles who were not attending church, simply because they felt a need to reach these young people for Christ. "We invited the singles to come to our house on Thursday nights. Some came once or twice and others came every week. They felt accepted, free to bring friends, and free to talk about everything. Over time we encouraged them to join us for Bible study on Sunday morning at the church. Many came; in fact, so many came that we had to start a second class!

"We planned picnics and parties at various places and overnights at our bay house. Some in the group had children, and we always included them in our activities. We were fortunate and grateful for the opportunity to share with many." Ellen pauses, then continues, "Everyone needs to be touched with love."

I think for a moment about Ellen's statement. Everyone needs to be touched with love. Such a simple thought, yet, it becomes a nugget of gold when spoken by a woman whose tranquil life has touched so many for Christ.

I find Ellen to be a master at removing herself from our conversation as she redirects our focus to those who attended the

Thursday night group. So I will allow you, the reader, the opportunity to listen to voices of some who came to the Arandall's home on Thursday nights, played games at Miller's Park, and boiled shrimp, played softball, and helped to build bonfires at the bay house on New Year's Eve.

BRENDA:

"It brings tears to my eyes today as I think about the unconditional love that Ellen made available to everyone in that group. Everything that Ellen said was uplifting, positive, and comforting. The Arendalls' house was always open. One of my favorite memories is a New Year's celebration that they had at their bay house. They had a trailer in the backyard where all the boys slept, and they housed the girls in the main house. The bay house was filled with those who might not have had anyone to celebrate with on New Year's Eve. At midnight they lit a huge bonfire with driftwood that had washed up on the beach."

DONNIE:

"This couple seemed to compliment each other in their teaching.

Ellen allowed J. T. to appear as the leader of the discussions, always supporting him and confirming him as the leader of their home and their marriage. At the same time, J. T. respected her opinions and seemed to hang on to her every word. Singles saw them as a couple and never as two individuals. When one spoke of the Arendalls, it was always, 'J. T. and Ellen.' They were the ultimate couple setting an example of how marriage should be."

PAULETTE:

"I had finished nursing school and probably was not attending Sunday School when Ellen invited me to come to her home on Thursday night. I agreed to come. The group that I met was a mixture of all ages. It soon became a close-knit group, like a support group, and I was happy being a part. Ellen was such a loving, positive, peaceful person. Jim and I started dating, as did several other couples who met on Thursday night at the Arendalls' house. Jim and I married and are now actively involved in the life of our church. We were just two of the 'Thursday Night Singles' who are now married couples."

BOB:

"I was a heathen wasting my life away when J. T. recruited me as a warm body to come to his home and meet with a group on Thursday night. He said Ellen needed a few men to balance out the group. I felt compelled to go since J. T. was my boss. Discussions did not always begin biblical in nature, though Ellen and J. T. always seemed to bring them back around by the end of the evening. The subject matter was always pertinent to the singles lifestyle, including issues on dating, finances, goals, and dreams—that sometimes included marriage. Some found mates and I found Christ as my personal Savior."

Who can measure the impact that this quiet, serene, unassuming woman has had on the lives of others? Ellen's lifestyle—though she sometimes colored outside the lines of tradition—allowed her to touch countless lives with the love of Christ. The impact of this innovative approach to meeting the needs of single adults lives today not only in the lives of those touched, but also in the church where this ministry continues to reach out—both in traditional and nontraditional ways to unique populations.

As I write this chapter America is dealing with the horrible aftermath of an attack by terrorists on Tuesday, September 11, 2001. We have many uncomfortable feelings.

And we wonder how can we feel serene today? The future of our country, our world, is uncertain. How can anyone of us feel secure today? But God speaks to me in this quiet moment, reminding me that my peace, my serenity, as Ellen's, come from His Son.

I am reminded of one of Ellen's favorite quotes:

"The greatest knowledge is to know the will of God.

The greatest achievement is to do the will of God."

Author Unknown

Today, though our country is reeling from shock and devastation, Ellen remains the rock and adds her message to the above quote:

"… The greatest achievement is to do the will of God, *and don't worry while you are doing it!"*

Ellen's Favorite Hymn

WHEN WE WALK WITH THE LORD

John H. Sammis

When we walk with the Lord In the light of His Word,
What a glory He sheds on our way!
While we do His good will, He abides with us still
And with all who will trust and obey.

Not a burden we bear, Not a sorrow we share,
But our toil He doth richly repay;
Not a grief or a loss, Not a frown or a cross,
But is blest if we trust and obey.

But we never can prove The delights of His love
Until all on the altar we lay;
For the favor He shows and the joy He bestows
Are for them who will trust and obey.

Then in fellowship sweet We will sit at His feet,
Or we'll walk by His side in the way;
What He says we will do, Where He sends we will go—
Never fear, only trust and obey.

Refrain:
Trust and obey, for there's no other way
To be happy in Jesus, But to trust and obey.

A Recipe From Ellen's Kitchen

SHRIMP CASSEROLE

Sauté in 1 stick margarine:

1 onion,

1/2 green pepper,

1 large can mushroom pieces, drained

Add: 3 cups cooked shrimp.

Prepare: One box Uncle Ben's Long Grain and Wild Rice.

Mix all ingredients together. Add two cans cream of chicken soup.

Put in a 9 x 13-inch baking dish and top with crushed Ritz crackers.

Dot with butter and bake at 350 degrees for 30 minutes.

NOTE FROM ELLEN: I like to add a can of sliced water chestnuts.

Ella
A Portrait of Prudence

"A simple man believes anything,
But a prudent man gives thought to his steps."

(Proverbs 14:15)

*O*n a beautiful spring morning I turn into a quiet neighborhood on the eastern shore of Mobile Bay and locate Ella's house. A winding drive leads me to her door. Nearby a feathered choir greets me from overhanging branches. The fragrance and beauty of the outside flowers almost overwhelm me. However, once inside, it is the startling combination of simplicity and complexity of this one called Ella that that amazes me.

In simple terms Ella quickly shares with me her salvation experience. "All we have to do is accept Him. And I did that when I was twelve years old. I have never doubted that He saved me, and He has always taken care of me." As her life's story unfolds, I begin to understand the depth of her wisdom and her prudent lifestyle.

Ella was born July 25, 1907, to Samuel and Ella Crane. Her father was a fisherman who supported the family by net fishing in Mobile Bay. He carried his catch by boat across Mobile Bay to the waterfront in downtown Mobile, Alabama, where he sold the fish to Southern Fish and Oyster Company.

When Ella was just six years old, her father died. The country was experiencing depressed times. Her young, widowed mother moved the family of eleven across Mobile Bay by boat to Stockton. With the help of a son who worked in a nearby veneer mill, the family survived by raising chickens, selling eggs, and planting and harvesting a garden each year. These early years impacted Ella. She learned about conserving, thrift, and planning for the future as her mother taught by example.

Words not often used in today's society, I think—conserving, thrift, planning for the future. When used by today's parents they have little meaning if parents portray a different lifestyle. Ella's mother taught her well. She taught by example. But I wonder what life was really like for Ella.

The petite lady across the table, dressed in white pants and soft orange shirt with matching lipstick, speaks freely about those years. I listen for traces of bitterness, hurt, or disappointment, but there are none. Rather, she verbalizes love for her mother who taught her to appreciate even the little things in life, something as insignificant as sugar. She expresses gratitude to a family living in Stockton, Alabama, the McMillans, who often invited the widow and her children to their home each year during the Christmas season. Words of appreciation for a Christian teacher, Mr. Pierce Mason, who influenced her life, are next on her list. "Mr. Mason encouraged me to read," she says. "He told us,

With the help of a son who worked in a nearby veneer mill, the family survived by raising chickens, selling eggs, and planting and harvesting a garden each year. These early years impacted Ella. She learned about conserving, thrift, and planning for the future as her mother taught by example.

'You can't tell a book by its cover.' He was a good teacher." And no doubt, Ella was a good student. Following the advice of this godly teacher and her own prudence and planning led to a high school graduation ceremony for Ella. She was one of four students who graduated from Stockton High School in 1928, a time when few women in the rural south achieved that lofty goal.

Ella left home to attend Twentieth Century Business College in Mobile and after graduation from business school she worked at F. C. Thomas Sash and Door Factory for two years. These were depression years and Ella, like thousands of others across the country, lost her job. Later Swift and Company, a meat packing house in Mobile, hired her. Ella walked to work six days each week. She stood while working her twelve-hour shift earning fifteen cents per hour. While earning the meager income of 10 dollars and 80 cents per week, she not only supported herself and contributed to the support of her large family, but also began to save. Displaying frugality, which remains her trademark today, she deposited money in the First National Bank in downtown Mobile each payday. "If you don't try to save, you won't have money to do what you need to do," Ella reminds me.

Such a simple concept, I think. Yet, it involves planning, thrift, common sense and judgment, virtues seldom seen in today's buy now-pay later society. Valuable nuggets of wisdom to be shared with today's woman.

Ella rarely thought of buying things for herself, but she loved Snickers candy bars and sometimes it was hard for her to pass up this treat. Prudence won out and instead she used the change to put coats on layaway at Grant's Department Store for her mother and a handicapped sister.

While Ella lived and worked in downtown Mobile, she met a handsome man named Joseph. Her thriftiness allowed Ella to do something important she wanted to do. She withdrew money from her bank account and purchased a lovely gown to wear when she said, "I do," to Joseph Guillot. Joseph earned the family income as an assistant engineer on an oil tanker during World War II. Ella never worked outside the home after her marriage, but she continued to live her conservative lifestyle. She invested in postal bonds, enabling the young couple to pay cash for a new home in the Toulminville area of Mobile.

Though the couple was not blessed with children, Joseph and Ella were afforded many opportunities to touch the lives of family members. "The Lord works things out," Ella says seriously. "When my brother's wife developed tuberculosis, Joe and I cared for their children for more than a year. If we had had children of our own, we might not have been able to help. God, in His wisdom, allowed me to be available to take care of those children."

I know there must be more, but I feel I should not ask. Ella had finished her story when she gave God the credit.

Later I talked with Ella's niece Jackie and asked if she had heard family stories about three children Joe and Ella kept while their mother was treated for tuberculosis. Jackie replied, "I have. I am one of the children!"

Jackie, the middle child, has no memories of the era when her father, along with three children under the age of four, moved in with Aunt Ella and Uncle Joe. "I have been told that all three of us were sick," Jackie said. "I had rickets and all of us had asthma. Many times we cried all night long." Jackie's love for her Aunt Ella was easily perceived in her voice and became more evident as she softly sobbed while sharing another touching story.

"Before I was born, my older brother was very ill. The doctor in Stockton told the family he had done all he could do for the infant and said 'he was at death's door.' He advised the family to take the baby to Mobile to a specialist. But my parents did not have any money. It was Aunt Ella and Uncle Joe that gave them the ten or fifteen dollars to pay the doctor and additional money to buy gas for us to drive to Mobile.

"Aunt Ella has taken care of many others in the family. Her sister, Dona, had polio as a child and was left handicapped. She lived with Aunt Ella and Uncle Joe for more than forty years. Aunt Ella has basically spent her entire life taking care of people."

After Joe was diagnosed with prostate cancer, Ella became his caregiver. "I asked the Lord to give me the strength to take care of him," Ella says. "And He did give me the strength I needed. I took care of him at home until one week before he died. One Monday afternoon he began to hallucinate—seeing things and talking about ships. In the early morning hours the next day he stopped talking. A nurse came to check on him, and we moved him to hospice care at Mercy Medical in Daphne. It was as if he just went to sleep and didn't wake up. He died a week later."

We sit quietly for a moment as sadness seems to pervade Ella's body. Yet, this remarkable one who speaks of her husband in soft tones and love quickly returns to the present and talks about her life after the death of her mate. She expresses thanks that she is financially comfortable. Having lived a life of thriftiness, Ella is now blessed with financial security.

There was never a time that Ella's lifestyle did not reflect her early commitment to Christ. She taught Sunday School for more than forty years, worked in Vacation Bible School and worked in the church nursery. Always busy, good stewards, both of money and of time, Joseph and Ella had helped establish Presbyterian churches in Mobile and Chickasaw.

Today she remains active in the church they attended prior to his death, Spanish Fort Presbyterian Church. At ninety-four she remains a faithful child of the Savior that she accepted more than eighty years ago. She continues to attend Sunday School, a mission circle, and is a member of the Banner Crew Ladies who hang banners in the chapel and sanctuary for Sunday services.

"It just doesn't seem right when I don't go to church on Sunday," Ella says. "It is my place of strength. I don't go for the preacher. I go to worship the Lord." It was no surprise to those who know her best when her church named Ella an honorary life member in Presbyterian Women.

During her lifetime Ella has worn an array of hats: career woman, wife, caregiver, nurse, Sunday School teacher, family matriarch, and seamstress. She sewed for her mother and sister as long as they lived. And most of her life she has made her own clothes, even suits and matching hats. "There was one twenty-year period in my life when I never bought a garment," Ella says. "I made everything that I wore."

But perhaps the hat that displays her thrift and frugality best today is her gardener's hat. It is in this arena of Ella's life that forethought, planning, and hard work is most evident. With the help of a nephew who tilled the soil, in the spring of 2001 Ella, at ninety-three years of age, planted a garden.

From where we are seated at her dinette table, I can see a large fenced area in the back yard. I tell Ella that her former neighbor and my friend told me that several years ago she gave him the biggest zucchini that he had ever seen.

"Well, my garden did not do too good this year," she exclaims. "I think it needs to be limed. But I still had plenty cucumbers, tomatoes, string beans, Irish potatoes, eggplant, peppers, and corn. We always have a dry spell in the summer and that hurts a garden. I usually freeze a lot, but I was gone twelve days during the summer, so I didn't get as much canning done. While I was gone, family members and neighbors gathered the vegetables. I just can't stand to see anything wasted.

"But the fall garden did better. The climate is better, so the garden does better. I had plenty carrots, collards, broccoli, cauliflower, and lettuce. Well, the lettuce really didn't come up as good as it does sometimes," she confides.

"I made jams and jellies—grape jam and jelly, blueberry jam and jelly, fig preserves, and pear honey." When Ella was finished with her jelly making she had grape juice and blueberry juice left but not enough of either to make a batch of jelly. So she mixed the two. She reminds me again, "I just can't stand to see things wasted."

"What do you do with all this jelly?" I ask. Her answer was as simple and complex as this woman I have grown to love.

"I give it away," she answers.

And, I think, Ella has given her entire life away to others. In her simplicity, she has discovered life's complex virtues. In her thriftiness she has "laid up treasures where moth and rust do not corrupt."

In living a life of prudence, Ella found the abundant life. Ninety-four years of golden wisdom—how remarkable!

Ella's Favorite Hymn

I COME TO THE GARDEN ALONE

C. Austin Miles

I come to the garden alone,
While the dew is still on the roses;
And the voice I hear,
Falling on my ear,
The Son of God discloses.

He speaks, and the sound of His voice
Is so sweet the birds hush their singing;
And the melody
That He gave to me,
Within my heart is ringing.

I'd stay in the garden with Him
Though the night around me be falling,
But He bids me go;
Through the voice of woe,
His voice to me is calling.

Chorus:
And He walks with me,
And He talks with me,
And He tells me I am His own,
And the joy we share as we tarry there,
None other has ever known.

A Recipe From Ella's Kitchen

DELMONICO CAKE

1 stick butter or margarine	1/2 cup vegetable shortening
2 cups sugar	5 egg yokes
1 teaspoon vanilla	
2 cups all-purpose flour (measure after sifting)	
1 teaspoon soda	1 cup buttermilk
1 cup shredded coconut	5 egg whites

In a large bowl cream butter and shortening. Gradually add sugar and beat until light and fluffy. Add egg yokes and vanilla and blend well. Sift flour and soda three times. Add to batter, alternating with buttermilk, beginning and ending with flour. Beat egg whites until stiff but not dry. Fold in batter with coconut. Bake in three greased and floured 10-inch pans at 350 degrees. Let stand about 10 minutes before removing from pans.

ICING

1-8 oz. package cream cheese, softened
1/2 stick butter or margarine, softened
1 pound box confectioner's sugar
1 cup chopped pecans or walnuts

In a small bowl beat cream cheese with butter until smooth. Gradually add sugar and nuts and beat well. Blend well and spread on cake layers' tops and sides.

NOTE FROM ELLA: I use about 1 1/2 cups of sugar and a little milk for the right spreading consistency.

Lib
A Portrait of Steadfastness

"Create in me a pure heart, O God,
and renew a steadfast spirit within me."

(Psalm 51:10)

On a sidewalk outside a palace in Istanbul, Turkey, Don and I followed a couple that stopped briefly to identify and admire plants bordering our pathway. I noticed a tree that looked as if it might be dying, and as the couple approached the tree, the lady turned to her husband and in a sweet southern style exclaimed, "Tom, I wish you would look! That is a southern magnolia tree and it is not a bit happy about where it is planted!"

I felt this fellow traveler must be someone special, concerned about the welfare of a tree, and I wished I knew her better.

Six years later I have the privilege of spending a delightful afternoon at this lady's house. Tom and Lib Dodd's comfortable home, built by Tom's family early in the twentieth century, is nestled near Highway 98 just outside Mobile, Alabama, amid endless rows of the family's nursery greenhouses. The drive I enter leads to a cobblestone-paved parking area. Lib invites me into her home and we sit at her kitchen table. We often sit at tables for nourishment. However, today, at Lib's house, in addition to my favorite nutritious snack (chocolate chip cookies) I am served a generous portion of love and an insight into the real meaning of steadfastness.

> "*But it was in the floral shop that I learned to work. There have been times in my life when I had to help out, and I could do whatever needed to be done, because I had been taught to work. I feel that God allowed me this opportunity to learn to work.*"

Born in Dothan, Alabama, in 1919 to Elizabeth and W. A. Pittman, Lib was christened in the Methodist church. Each Sunday her father took her to Sunday School. At the age of 10 she accepted Jesus as her Savior and made her public profession of faith, presenting herself to the church for membership.

"I think my father's faithfulness and his positive attitude shaped my life," Lib says. "He taught me to be honest. Soon after I started driving I had a little accident and bent a fender on our car. When he asked how it happened, I could have said that I didn't know, but instead I told the truth. I knew if I told the truth, it would be all right. And it was."

Lib's beloved father became ill during her freshman year at Athens College. Her mother needed her so she returned to Dothan to help in the family business, a floral shop. "I think back on the many times He has taken care of me in special ways," Lib interjects as if she is thinking aloud. "I hated the floral shop. My mother put me in a corner when I was five years old to keep me out of mischief. This was the era before florist-picking machines were invented. I had to sit there and wire fern all day.

"But it was in the floral shop that I learned to work. There have been times in my life when I had to help out, and I could do whatever needed to be done, because I had been taught to work. I feel that God allowed me this opportunity to learn to work."

What wisdom! Many who experience the early death of a parent turn from their faith or, perhaps, blame God, while Lib expresses gratitude for the growth she experienced while toiling beside her mother.

"One thing I decided during this time: If I ever got married, I would marry a man that did not know a rose from a petunia!" Lib goes on to explain, "I met Tom at the Alabama Nursery and Florist Convention. I was the only girl there, so Tom asked me for a date. That same year, in the fall, I went to the Georgia/Auburn football game in Columbus, Georgia. Tom's brother, Bill, had a date with a friend of mine. Back then we wore hats and high-heeled shoes and flowers to the games. Tom walked up and said, 'That's a pretty carnation you are wearing.' But it wasn't a carnation; it was a mum. I recalled my earlier vow that I would not marry a man who knew anything about flowers. I thought God might be trying to tell me something."

A courtship began to flourish between Lib and Tom. He proposed the following April, and they were married in July— less than a year after they met.

When I comment that they had known each other less than a year when they married, Lib smiles sweetly and says, "I think it will last. We have been married more than sixty years."

In 1920 Tom's family built the home where we sit today and where Lib and Tom have lived for over fifty years. They reared their four children here. "We lost our son Bobby," Lib says. "Bobby always said he wanted to be an engineer. I though he meant an engineer on a train. But he finished at Auburn with a degree in civil engineering and went to work for Florida Light and Power Company at a time when civil engineers were in demand."

In her soft sweet voice Lib talks about her son's death. "He died at thirty-six years of age with melanoma. God knows what is best. The minute Tom told me, I felt God's presence close to me."

I think how privileged I am to sit today with one who trusts completely and remains steadfast in spirit even during the darkest times. And I wonder—will I, will you, the reader, allow these words of wisdom to bring change to our hearts and our lives? When we experience difficult times, will we seek His presence?

Steadfast in her commitment to Christ as a young woman, Lib faithfully attended the Methodist church. And after her marriage, steadfast in her love for her husband Tom, she joined his church, First Baptist, Semmes, and was immersed in Big Creek. Later the family joined Spring Hill Baptist Church in Mobile. Here Lib and Tom faithfully work and worship today.

At Semmes First Baptist Church Lib began working with girls and young women though the missions programs, Girls Auxiliary, and Young Woman's Auxiliary. "I loved them and they also loved me," she says. "I felt like I was accomplishing something." And she was accomplishing much. For many years, solid in faith, faithful in service, she taught these impressionable minds, shaping their lives in special ways.

"You might describe me as tenacious," Lib volunteers, "persistent, or even stubborn."

Rather, I see this Christian woman steadfastly marching toward goals. Whether shaping the lives of children at church or organizing forces to make things happen in the community, wherever Lib is, she is at the center, a moving force, making things happen.

The Camellia Festival was an annual fund-raiser for the local schools when Lib and Tom's children were young. Lib was cochairman nearly every year. "This was a big event, a big deal,"

Lib recalls. "A king and queen were selected from the elementary, middle, and the high school. There were huge displays of camellias every year. One year we even erected brick walls inside the gym to create a garden effect."

But it was a six-year restoration project, the one-room schoolhouse that Tom attended as a child, that became Lib's passion. "It was Lib's idea to rescue the building," my friend Carolyn told me later. "Lib said that we had already let too much history slip away and that we had to take a stand and rescue the building." The building was a cedar-shingled, rundown one-room school built in 1901. In the early years it housed grades one through six. In recent years the building was moved from its original location to be used as the school counselor's office.

The Semmes Women's Club sponsored the first meeting and the project quickly became a community-wide effort. "Our timetable is not always God's timetable," Lib says. "But if we just stick with something, eventually it will happen. For an entire year my dining table was piled high with pictures, papers, and books. Once each week a crowd arrived to work on the first of many fund-raisers, a scrapbook of memories. We found a leader, an accountant, Joe Shumock."

The group wanted to restore the school, built almost one hundred years ago for a total of 350 dollars, to its original state. The first architect the group hired wanted electricity in the building for lighting and air-conditioning. "Absolutely not!" Lib said. "If we change much we lose the value." She wanted a building to allow today's children to experience school life in the atmosphere their grandparents and great-grandparents had been schooled.

Thanks to the dedication of this persistent woman, and many others who worked, pledged money, and dreamed the dream, today that dream is a reality. The one-room school has been restored and moved back to the original location. It is available today for field trips. There children experience "A Day of School in the 1900s."

"Would you like to see the school?" Lib asks.

"Can we go today?" I am concerned that the building would be locked late in the afternoon. I want to go inside.

"I have a key," Lib says.

Tom walks with us as we wind through the nursery property to the school. I step through the door and simultaneously step back one hundred years in time. "Blackboards," literally boards painted black found during the renovation process, are still covered with chalk messages from the earlier era. There is no electricity; oil lamps provide the necessary illumination.

Education and preserving history are important to Lib. In every area of her life she has demonstrated steadfastness with a golden spiritual thread woven into every fabric. Pictures from the past reveal a white chapel sitting beside the school with a row of small oak trees between the buildings. Although the church was torn down many years ago, the committee built a replica of that church, Semmes Baptist, now known as First Baptist Church, Semmes. It stands on the other side of the now huge gnarled oaks, a symbolic recognition of the spiritual component of a complete education.

The Dodds have a reputation for generosity not only in their community but also throughout the area and the state. I mention this to Lib and she smiles sweetly and redirects the conversation.

"You cannot outgive God," she insists.

But others have shared the particulars, talking of the beautiful beds of plants at Auburn University and countless other campuses, myriad's of azaleas and flowering shrubs that grace the grounds of Spring Hill Baptist Church and other churches throughout Alabama. A special azalea, "The Kate Arendall" named many years ago for the pastor's wife at Dauphin Way Baptist Church, is planted in the yards of countless preachers' homes and on many church lawns.

Christmas time finds Lib in many places but most often at her church. She works alongside groups of women, young, and old, who fashion fresh greenery into wreaths for the church. As I write in late December, those wreaths are hanging.

I recall the words Lib spoke earlier this season. "You cannot outgive God. One of the nicest things about growing old is that we can look back on so many times that our Heavenly Father has taken care of us. My generation was so blessed to have been depression children. We learned the value of work. Today's children should find work they really enjoy—and then stick with it!"

What a challenge for today's woman from a steadfast sister in Christ, I think. Find your place, hold fast, and make a difference.

Lib's Favorite Hymn

JESUS LOVES ME

Anna B. Warner

Jesus loves me! this I know,
For the Bible tells me so;
Little ones to Him belong,
They are weak, but He is strong.

Jesus loves me! He who died
Heaven's gate to open wide:
He will wash away my sin,
Let His little child come in.

Jesus loves me! loves me still,
Though I'm very weak and ill;
From His shining throne on high,
Comes to watch me where I lie.

Jesus loves me! He will stay
Close beside me all the way,
If I love Him when I die
He will take me home on high.

Chorus:

Yes, Jesus loves me!
Yes, Jesus loves me!
Yes, Jesus loves me!
The Bible tells me so.

A Recipe From Lib's Kitchen

CANDIED ORANGE PEEL—
A RECIPE FROM THE DEPRESSION ERA

Scrape pulp from peel of 3 or 4 oranges.
(You will get neater petals if oranges are cut lengthwise.)

Cover peel with I tablespoon salt in 4 cups of water.
Weight with a plate to keep peel under water. Let stand overnight.
Drain and wash thoroughly.

Next, cover with cold water; heat to boiling.
Drain. Repeat this 3 times.

With kitchen scissors, cut into petal-shaped strips.
Put 2 cups petals into saucepan, and add 2 cups sugar and
1/2 cup water. Stir until sugar dissolves.

Cook slowly until peel is translucent, about 30 minutes. Drain,
then roll in granulated sugar. Dry on cake rack.

Hint: Put cake rack on waxed paper to catch drips.

Meta
A Portrait of Devotion

---

*O*utside the sky is overcast: the air is muggy. Inside the room
is sunny, cheerful, and inviting, alive with color. On the
outside of Meta's door hangs a patriotic fall wreath in recognition
of victims of the September 11, 2001, terrorist attacks. Inside I
discover a collage made with recent pictures of family members
from oldest to youngest. But immediately my attention is drawn
to a portrait of the Willis family, husband and wife surrounded by
sons, daughters, and grandchildren. The family was photographed
to commemorate the golden wedding anniversary of James and
Meta Willis. Though her perfectly coiffured hair is snow-white,
the face of Meta, the family matriarch, belies the passing of ten

years since that anniversary celebration.

Born to Eva and John Moody in 1922, Meta recalls going as a child to a Baptist church where her mother played the piano for worship services. The young Meta was touched by and even shaped by those early experiences. But it was much later, after she was married and had children, when she met her Master.

A pastor, Rev. Nolan Futral, visited the couple in their home during the critical illness of a daughter, Deborah. He not only comforted the family of an ill child, he introduced the couple to Christ. Meta and Jim joined Indian Springs Church of God near Mobile, Alabama (known today as Pathway Temple), and faithfully attended as long as their health permitted.

"Whatever we did, we wanted to do it well," Meta says. So for many years, in addition to their "on the job" training, she and her husband attended "Singing Schools," denominational training for church musicians. Meta approached every task, whether playing the piano or covering a canvas with oils, with zeal and intensity.

While visiting with her grandmother during summer months Meta taught herself to play the organ. She never had a music lesson, but their church was in need of musicians. Rev. Futral approached Jim and Meta and the couple agreed to help. For the next twenty-five years Jim directed the music for the worship services, while Meta accompanied on the piano.

"Our pastor helped us to grow," Meta says. "He and his wife became our dearest friends. My husband taught Sunday School for about thirty years. He was a man of great wisdom." The devotion Meta had for her husband is obvious as she speaks.

"Whatever we did, we wanted to do it well," Meta says. So for many years, in addition to their "on the job" training, she and her husband attended "Singing Schools," denominational training for church musicians. Meta approached every task, whether playing the piano or covering a canvas with oils, with zeal and intensity.

I think how different today's world would be if everyone wanted to do his or her best in every situation. What differences would we see if only Christians would give their best? How would my world, or your world, be different if each of us did our best each time we faced a task?

This simple bit of wisdom has unlimited potential for today's woman!

There were seven children born into the Willis home. "We all worked together," Meta says. "I never had any desire to be famous. I never worked a day in my life outside my home. I just wanted to be home with my children, to be a home-maker."

Meta was there with the children to send them off to school each day and greet them when they returned. She cooked two hot meals—

"*I* taught my children that honesty takes care of a lot of things. And I taught them that they should not argue and fight. There were few arguments in our home," Meta says. "It is a big waste of time when families argue and fight, and we don't need to waste valuable time."

breakfast and the evening meal—which was always ready when Jim arrived from work each afternoon at 5:30 P.M. Sunday dinner was served in the dining room with the dining table covered with a lace cloth and the best dishes. Meta arose early and prepared the entire meal before leaving for church, unless they were having fried chicken. Chicken was always fried after returning home and served hot. Meta loved having all the family around her table. After the children married they returned home for Sunday dinner bringing spouses and grandchildren.

Her love for family was demonstrated not only at mealtime but also throughout the day and into the evening. There was never a television in the Willis home. Daylight hours found children playing outside. Many nights after dinner the family gathered and played games. The children were learning more than the rules of Monopoly and dominoes. Meta was teaching them, informally, the rules of life.

"I taught my children that honesty takes care of a lot of things. And I taught them that they should not argue and fight. There were few arguments in our home," Meta says. "It is a big waste of time when families argue and fight, and we don't need to waste valuable time."

Words of wisdom practiced by an earlier generation offer a timely message for today's parents.

Every morning each of the children—Brenda, Jimmy, Sharon, Billy, Deborah, Paul, and Mark—was prayed for aloud by their father before he left for work. Anticipating his arrival home in the afternoon, Meta met him at door where he hugged her and kissed her. "He never demanded much," her daughter Deborah volunteered, "but she gave him her everything."

On one occasion what initially appeared to be a minor injury led to a forty-day hospitalization for Jim. "I was always there, at his side, encouraging him, praying for him and—after he began to recover—pushing his I.V. pole and walking beside him," Meta says.

"Walking beside him," I think, a simple but beautiful word picture of the devotion in marriage.

Retirement years found Meta and Jim walking together as they gardened. Meta and Jim worked side-by-side in the garden every day of the season until the midday southern heat forced them inside. They gardened organically—consulting the almanac and the position of the moon. Meta helped Jim punch holes twelve inches apart in garden hoses to use for irrigation. She helped him plant and later harvest the ripened vegetables. "They grew the biggest and best tomatoes in the south, about one-thousand pounds one year," Deborah said.

The ripened tomatoes that were not eaten were sold in an interesting manner. Meta would set a table in front of their house near the road then hammer a sign into the ground nearby: "Tomatoes for Sale." If she was busy inside or not at home, people would stop, weigh the tomatoes they wanted to buy and leave money in a bowl provided for them. Meta used the money for gifts, many for her beloved husband.

During warm summer months one could often find the couple sitting in the porch swing by late afternoon. The swing faced the garden and Jim sat with his arm around Meta's neck while Meta's hand rested on his leg. Occasionally the tranquillity was interrupted briefly as one gave the other a gentle pat.

Sensing the strong bond and extreme devotion that existed in their marriage, I ask what advice Meta might have for young couples today. "Respect," she says. "Respect is the key to marriage. And both partners need to be committed to their church and to the Lord."

A simple statement with a clear message. When two are committed to each other and to God, strength from beside, and from above, gently guides them through difficult times.

Additional medical challenges loomed on the horizon and difficult times returned. The couple had already experienced the deaths of two children, a son sixteen years old, and an adult daughter, each dying with cancer. Jim survived heart surgery and colon cancer. Later cancer struck the family and Meta sat beside her dying husband, and held his hand and said, "Let go and go to be with Jesus. The children will take care of me."

"When I lost him, I lost everything," Meta says. "He was my rock and everybody's rock. There has not been a day that has passed since his death that I have not missed him." Tears spill from her eyes as she speaks.

Yet Meta filled her days following Jim's death with creative projects extending beyond the keyboard that she taught herself to play. Craft projects and writing poetry and words and music for songs kept her busy. At the request of Jimmie Davis, former governor of Louisiana, Meta and a friend, Gordan Bellcase, transcribed to paper the music from a recording he made. She taught herself to paint with oils and admits that of all the things she taught herself to do, painting was the activity she enjoyed most.

The area of her life in which her devotion is most obvious is in her faithfulness to the Word of God. "I read a lot," Meta volunteers. I ask what she was reading and expected a simple answer. Rather, I am startled by her reply. "I read the Bible every day. When I wake up each morning, I tell myself I will read just two hours. But often when I have read two hours, I just cannot quit. The stories are so interesting that I cannot put my Bible down."

For the past ten years Meta has been confined to bed following several strokes. The cheerful room where we visit is not located in the home where she reared her children. We visit in Room 312 at Beverly Health Care in Mobile, Alabama.

I hear no complaints this afternoon as I visit with Meta in the nursing home. To the contrary, I hear her say repeatedly, "I am just thankful for what I can do. I try to do everything that I can do."

One of the things Meta continues to do is write music. "I have one in my head now," she says. "It's not on paper yet." But I learn there are many poems that *are* on paper.

Meta's life, like the following poem that she wrote, *Reflections*, challenges each of us to look upward toward a higher calling, a new level of devotion.

REFLECTIONS

Meta Willis

Do you ever stop and wonder
Who you most would imitate,
How you'd like to be remembered
and the qualities you relate?

How do you size up and can you be
A trustworthy and honest friend,
And will you be remembered
As a person on whom one can depend?

When they ask for you to pray for a loved one
Do you leave feeling it was done?
Or do you soon forget that you promised
And go on to another one?

Can you truly say you love Jesus
In all that you say and do,
Does your life reflect Christian living,
Can others see Jesus in you?
Make sure that your life is a mirror
And help all to know and see,
That the reflection they most often see there
Will be of Jesus and not of you and me.

Meta's Favorite Hymn

WHEN HE WAS ON THE CROSS (I WAS ON HIS MIND)

Mike Payne and Ronnie Hinson

I am not on an ego trip
I'm nothing on my own
I make mistakes, I often slip
Just common flesh and bone
But I'll prove someday just what I say
I'm of a special kind
For when He was on the cross
I was on His mind.

A look of love was on His face
The thorns were on His head
The blood was on His scarlet robe
Til it stained it crimson red
Though His eyes were on the crown that day
He looked ahead in time
When He was on the cross
I was on His mind.

CHORUS
He knew me, yet He loved me
He whose glory made the heaven's shine
So unworthy of such mercy
Yet when He was on the cross
I was on his mind.

A Recipe From Meta's Kitchen

FUDGE SCOTCHIE SQUARES

1/2 cup graham cracker crumbs

1 cup Eagle Brand sweetened condensed milk

1 small package chocolate chip morsels

1 small package butterscotch morsels

1 cup English walnuts or pecans

Mix all ingredients together and press in well-greased 10 x 13-inch pan. Bake at 350 degrees 30–35 minutes.

"B"

A Portrait of Beauty

"Finally, brothers, whatever is true, whatever is noble,
whatever is right, whatever is pure, whatever is lovely . . .
think about such things."

(Philippians 4:8)

The white blossoms of sprawling apple trees provided springtime umbrellas that shaded tender bedding plants from the sun. Later the trees' leaves softened rains that pelted fragile summer petals. A trimmed hedge formed the background for the informal garden ablaze with color during summer months.

Young Annie Boyd Parker lived next door to the flower garden. She often walked a well-worn path from her back door across her lawn and followed the hedge that led to the back door of a large white house. Here her grandmother lived. Though the youngster loved being enveloped by the beauty of the garden, she was not free to cut flowers at will. On Saturday afternoons, under the supervision of her grandmother, she was allowed to choose, cut, and arrange the Sunday flowers in a crystal vase for her grandmother's house. Perhaps it was in this garden amid apple blossoms, flowering shrubs, and roses that her lifelong love for beauty, not only for flowers but also for all things beautiful, was birthed and nurtured.

Annie Boyd was born April 17, 1920 to Henry Grady and Irene Riggins Parker. "Although we lived next door to my grandmother, two aunts, and an uncle, my brother and I never felt that we were spoiled; we just felt loved," she says. "Two things they gave us were opportunities and love."

Growing up in Talladega, Alabama, she was called Annie B, which in college was shortened to just "B." It is a simple, yet unique and distinguishing name for the beautiful lady with whom I sit today in her home on the eastern shore of Mobile Bay.

Her family worshiped at First Baptist Church and the church supported a strong youth program. It was in this nurturing environment that "B" began to understand the importance of God in her life. At twelve years of age she made her profession of faith and was baptized. Each summer with her youth group she attended the Baptist assemblies at nearby Shocco Springs. There in conferences and inspirational services of worship she was challenged to make a deeper commitment. "It was at Shocco Springs at fifteen years of age that I made a decision to do whatever God called me to do," "B" says.

After high school graduation "B" was off to Alabama College for Women (now the University of Montevallo). She became involved in campus activities as well as the Baptist Student Union on a local and state level. One emphasis of the BSU in those days was the encouragement to move your church membership to a church in your college community. She joined Montevallo Baptist Church. A Christ-centered upbringing, early church experiences, her college days, and working in the secular world during World War II are all factors "B" recognizes today as God's way of preparing her for a life of service.

"B's" life picture unfolded dramatically when she was in her late twenties. In 1945 the Alabama Women's Missionary Union employed her as Baptist Student Union director at Alabama College. Shortly thereafter Howard College (now Samford University) in Birmingham employed a young man to fill a similar position on that campus. He was William K. Weaver Jr., who had grown up in Talladega and was the big brother of her dear friend Ann Weaver. In their work Bill and "B" were often together in meetings and conferences.

An amusing incident occurred on one occasion when she had invited him to be a speaker at a banquet on her campus. Bill's traveling companion that night was a student from Howard. He later related to "B" the anxiety Bill felt because he had failed to bring a corsage for "B." But when they walked into the banquet room she was wearing a beautiful orchid, a flower from her date for the evening. Later, while telling "B" this story, their friend commented, "I think Bill had begun to think of you as being more than just a friend and coworker."

> "*A* deep love exists between the two of us. We have always had an assurance that we were meant to be together," "B" says quietly. Today, more than fifty-three years after their wedding, I see his face light up when she enters the room.

And the friend was right. "The 1948 Student Conference at

Ridgecrest Baptist Assembly in North Carolina, and my invitation to ride back to Alabama with Bill and two friends, were turning points in our long friendship," "B" says. Throughout the summer Bill's job-related travel throughout the state included frequent detours by way of Montevallo to visit with her. By summer's end a proposal had been spoken and a ring given. On November 4, 1948, in Montevallo Baptist Church, "B" became Mrs. William K. Weaver.

"A deep love exists between the two of us. We have always had an assurance that we were meant to be together," "B" says quietly. Today, more than fifty-three years after their wedding, I see his face light up when she enters the room.

Early in their marriage "B" began to experience severe pain in her back. The pain quickly increased in intensity and four months later a Birmingham physician discovered a tumor in her spinal column that required immediate surgery, a surgery that might have prevented "B" from ever walking again. "The doctor was ecstatic when I wiggled my toes following the surgery," "B" says. Though the tumor was benign, radiation treatments followed the surgery and there was concern the couple might not have children.

Another part of God's plan for this couple was revealed when Bill was called as pastor of First Baptist Church, Sylacauga, Alabama, in 1950. "Major moves were traumatic to me," "B" says. "We were dealing with my recovery and the possibility of never conceiving a child. But God called and we went." With a smile on her beautiful face she whispers, "God blessed us as we followed His will. You cannot imagine our almost unbelievable excitement when tests confirmed my pregnancy. A precious baby daughter, our only child, was born nine months after our move to Sylacauga. We named her Anne."

The ten years in Sylacauga were rewarding and happy years. God promises to bless those who are faithful to Him. The Weaver family was faithful, but soon they were faced with another challenge.

Mobile College (now the University of Mobile) was only a bold vision in 1961 when Dr. William K. Weaver Jr. was named to lead in the establishment of a new college. In the fall of that year Mobile College was chartered and in September 1963 began offering classes. "This institution was meant to be," "B" says emphatically. "When Bill was named president I knew it was my role to support him and be a part of this new endeavor. We saw miracles happen there." Today, in retirement years, her enthusiasm for the college remains contagiously genuine as she reminisces about the early days.

Those who came as faculty members were strangers to each other. "B" thought of having a Christmas party as a way for families to get acquainted. The party became a tradition. The seated dinner was held at the president's home with Christmas greens creating a festive atmosphere. After dinner formality was replaced with frivolity. Faculty members brought an ornament for the Christmas tree the first year they attended the party. The birth of each faculty baby was commemorated with a special ornament placed on the tree by the Weavers and another ornament was sent home as a gift to the baby. Guests shared inexpensive gifts and much laughter was heard. "B's" desires were fulfilled as she watched the faculty family bond and form lifelong friendships.

The impact "B" had on college events during those days is immeasurable. She wanted every event to be special, properly done and with a different flair. She did this with her creative skills. Tissue-paper butterflies attached to thin wires might float above lovely arrangements on tables covered with lime green bedspreads but when more formality was required, the setting was carefully prepared. Her love for flowers and her talent for creating beautiful arrangements were shared unselfishly with others. "B's" commitment to do her best was a commitment to her Savior.

"Whatever I did, I wanted it to be special for Him," she says.

A friend recalls a state meeting held at the college. "B" was present and, as usual, was the gracious hostess. He remembers being in the banquet room where several students were helping to prepare for a luncheon. After the tables were set and the centerpieces in place, one student was heard whispering to another, "We'd better check with Miss "B" to make sure everything is just right!" She was their tender

"I had the most fantastic role models," Anne said. "My grandparents, my father, and my mother. My parents involved me in their lives. One might say, my mother trained me as I observed her behavior. In every situation, whether it was for others, or for me, she wanted it to be beyond the ordinary."

teacher, their mentor, and their friend.

I realize the wisdom "B" displayed as she involved young college women in beautiful events. And I admire the patience she exemplified as she quietly taught them to give their best efforts, accomplish the larger goal, and make it special for Him. Nuggets of wisdom that need to be shared!

On another occasion an open house for a new girls' dormitory was scheduled. In making a final check before visitors arrived, "B" felt that some of the bathrooms needed further attention. With a chuckle she says, "Sometimes it takes a little elbow grease to have things right. If it needs to be done, and time is a factor, you just do it. I live in a place that is attractive and cared for, and I wanted our visitors to know that we wanted the same for the girls who were moving into the dormitory."

Many have a "B" story to share. Her daughter, Anne, has many. "I had the most fantastic role models," Anne said. "My grandparents, my father, and my mother. My parents involved me in their lives. One might say, my mother trained me as I observed her behavior. In every situation, whether it was for others, or for me, she wanted it to be beyond the ordinary. Our extended family recognized her gifts and relied on her for help with large family gatherings.

"Mother loved planning and directing weddings as a pastor's wife and when needed, helping students at the college prepare for their weddings. Some years ago she began making bridal handkerchiefs as special remembrances for young friends," Anne said. When the hand-stitched gift is finished, one corner is embroidered with the bride's monogram and date. A letter of encouragement accompanies each gift and includes the thought that the bride's daughter might carry this same handkerchief on her wedding day, adding her own monogram and nuptial date.

"I have wonderful memories of my wedding," Anne said. "Mother organized everything. She designed in her mind and made for me an exquisite dress with a cathedral train and a lovely veil. I recall trying on a sleeve and mother carefully measuring the lace attachment so it would fall across my hand at just the right place. She wanted to make sure it was just right.

"And Mother designed and made beautiful robes of chiffon and lace to be worn by my two grandmothers when they died," Anne said. "It was her way of expressing one more time the love and appreciation she felt for each."

Though it has been more than seventeen years since the Weavers' retirement from the school, "B's" touch remains. I returned to the campus yesterday. Huge oak trees planted forty years ago line the entranceway forming a green canopy for all that enter—a vision of the first president of the college auxiliary organized by "B." I asked Mack Clark, Dean of the College of Arts and Sciences, to tell me more about "B."

"When I think of "B" I think of quality and beauty," he replied. "Whatever she did had quality. Everybody in town thought she was a beautiful person!" Mack recently redecorated the reception area of the Thomas T. Martin Fine Arts Building. He assembled exquisite furnishings either purchased or donated during "B's" time at the school—a fitting tribute to the former First Lady of Mobile College.

During retirement years "B" remains as active as her health permits. The Weavers continue to worship in the church they joined soon after moving to Mobile. And, as always, "B" finds herself helping to make things beautiful as she serves on the building and grounds committee and as an ex-officio member of the flower committee, a committee she chaired for more than twenty years. "I feel my church, every church, should be well cared for and tastefully decorated", "B" says. "For it is there we gather in the sanctuary each Sunday to meet Him for a special time of worship."

On special occasions "B" wears a pin attached to the shoulder of her dress. The beautiful gold-and-diamond-studded bee was a gift from her husband many years ago. That pin not only symbolizes "B's" nickname but also her busy life of helping and inspiring others.

The call of God she felt years ago has led to many unexpected avenues of service. "B's" life has touched family and friends, churches, and a college, as well as the communities where she has lived...and everything she touched was made more beautiful.

"B's" Favorite Hymn

AMAZING GRACE

John Newton

Amazing grace! how sweet the sound
That saved a wretch like me!
I once was lost, but now am found;
Was blind, but now I see.

'Twas grace that taught my heart to fear,
And grace my fears relieved;
How precious did that grace appear,
The hour I first believed!

Through many dangers, toils, and snares,
I have already come;
'Tis grace hath brought me safe thus far,
And grace will lead me home.

When we've been there ten thousand years,
Bright shining as the sun,
We've no less days to sing God's praise
Than when we'd first begun.

A Recipe From "B's" Kitchen

SCALLOPED OYSTERS

1 pint standard oysters
Saltine crackers, crumbled (about 1/2 pound)
Butter or margarine
2 cups finely chopped celery, sautéed
Rich chicken broth
2 eggs

Wash oysters. Put a layer of crumbled crackers on bottom of buttered casserole, then a layer of oysters, a sprinkle of salt and pepper, bits of butter and some of the sautéed celery. Cover with crumbled crackers. Add second layer of oysters, butter, sautéed celery and seasonings. Pour enough broth over all to moisten crackers well. Let stand for 5 minutes to allow broth to be absorbed. Add more broth as is necessary to make the crackers soggy. Bake at 350 degrees for about 30 minutes until well set and lightly browned. Beat two eggs well, pour over top and return to oven to brown. Serve piping hot. Serves 4 to 6.

From the famous Purefoy Hotel
Talladega, Alabama
1920-1961

Lillie
A Portrait of a Servant Heart

"Remember the words of the Lord Jesus, how he said,
'It is more blessed to give than to receive'."

(Acts 20: 35, KJV)

*O*n a Saturday night in April 1936, a group of church young people met for a fellowship at El Bethel Baptist Church in Greer, South Carolina. They had planned a romantic evening, which included the game "Pass the Thimble." The gentlemen stood in line waiting for their turn to take a walk with a partner while the young ladies formed a circle and passed a thimble.

When the signal was given to "Stop!" Lillie opened her hand to display the thimble she was holding. Delight was obvious on the face of the first gentleman in line: twenty-two-year-old, tall and handsome Lenhardt Roper. He smiled, reached for Lillie's hand and said, "Let's take that walk." Those were the initial steps in the couple's sixty-three-year journey of love.

Lillie Bell Phillips was born August 9, 1916, to farming parents, John and Emma Barker Phillips. Early years were spent near Easley, South Carolina. The family of fifteen lived in a large farmhouse surrounded by apple orchards and cotton fields and space for raising cows and chickens. Each child had specific responsibilities. Lillie and her older sister Gladys were responsible for keeping the front and back yards clean using brush brooms made from dogwood limbs. Often the girls carried cool water to family members working in the cotton fields. They carried milk and butter, in big buckets covered with lids, to a nearby spring for cooling and storage. It was in this setting, still young and tender, Lillie began to develop the heart of a servant.

The children walked one mile to the schoolhouse and a second mile as they returned each day. But the Phillips family was a two-vehicle family long before the term was coined. "I remember going to church in a wagon with Mother holding John," Lillie says. "As many of the children as could find room sat on blankets. The others rode in a carriage driven by one of my older brothers. Mules were hitched to the wagon; horses were hitched to the buggy." Often the preacher and his family ate Sunday lunch at the Phillips' home, a place always open to anyone needing a place to eat or to stay.

In this farming community of rural South Carolina young people usually gathered at the church for their social activity. Occasionally parties were held at someone's home. "One time the social was at our house," Lillie says. "The girls had to bake cakes or pies. We had a cakewalk and games and we had a good time."

Formal schooling, a strong work ethic, and influencing the children spiritually were important to Lillie's parents. Her father served as a deacon. Lillie's childhood memories are dotted with images of her mother kneeling as she prayed for each child by name. Life was stable, good, but suddenly while the three youngest children, including Lillie, were still in school, tragedy struck.

"Daddy got sick. He had flu and pneumonia and died at home," Lillie says. "My brother Truman had recently returned from service. He was enrolled in college, planning to become a preacher. Truman stepped up to our father's place at the table." Eleven days after his father's death, Truman died from injuries received in an automobile accident.

One can only imagine the responsibility this young widow felt toward her three youngest children. She was protective of the girls, but they were allowed to date at church socials. It was in this setting on that full-moon Saturday night in 1936 that Lillie, the young Christian woman with a thimble, joined hands with Lenhardt Roper. The next week may have been the longest of Lenhardt's life as he anticipated their first real date. Six weeks later they joined hands in marriage and walked together for more than six decades.

Those first years were spent in South Carolina as the couple welcomed two sons and their only daughter, Melba. Lenhardt joined the National Guard in 1941. After completing a government shipbuilding course, he was sent to Mobile, Alabama, where he worked for Gulf Shipbuilding Company and later, International Paper Company. Four more children were born to the Ropers in Mobile. In all they reared and educated six sons and a daughter.

The family first joined Bethany Baptist Church. Later they helped build Ninth Street Baptist Church in Prichard where they worshiped faithfully and sang in the church choir.

Though Lillie worked briefly, Lenhardt provided most of the family income as Lillie, patterning her days after her Savior, lived her life in service for others. She prayed daily for each of her seven children by name: Donald, Gerald, Melba, Pat, Douglas, Mike, and Royce. And by example and instruction she pointed each child toward Christ.

One Sunday morning when Mike was a baby, Lillie walked forward during a church service, placed her youngest child on the altar, and dedicated him to God. She had favorite lines that she quoted to the children, "Remember *who* you are and *whose* you are." Frequently she reminded them to: "Find your place and do your best." The entire family was talented musically and each child "found that place" in music, singing together as a family at home and in music evangelism, teaching voice, directing church music, singing solos, and faithfully singing in church choir cantatas.

"Mom could have been a great soloist, but she choose to sing with her family at home and in the church choir," Melba says. "Or she might have been a schoolteacher but she chose to teach young children in Sunday School and mission activities. Or perhaps she could have been a writer or a poet, but instead she enjoyed the poetry of life. Mom painted and might have been a great painter, but she chose to sketch nature scenes and draw pictures of brides wearing gowns for her granddaughters."

Sunday dinner, always a special meal, became an extended family tradition at the Ropers' house. One after another of the children married, and those who remained in Mobile always brought their families back home for Sunday dinner. Lillie prepared even larger Sunday meals of roast, fried chicken, rice, and gravy, as well as potatoes, vegetables, and always banana pudding. She was happiest when her family was together and she was serving them at her table.

Holidays, Thanksgiving, and Christmas, were special to Lillie. She spent days preparing everyone's favorite dishes and desserts. She loved being surrounded by family in the tiny Roper home filled with children, spouses, and grandchildren. Lillie never ate until she was certain that everyone else was served. Only then would she fill her own plate.

A simple, yet golden act of service, I think—observing carefully, watching for opportunities to serve, always putting others first.

After dinner on Christmas Eve the grandchildren and great-grandchildren opened the gifts stacked under the tree, a tradition Lillie would not let die. Yet one year she insisted her family not bring a gift for her. Rather, she asked that they begin to bring a picture ornament of each grandchild to hang on her Christmas tree. In time the tree was full of pictures.

Lillie often mentioned she wished she had one framed picture that included a picture of every family member. Gerald collected family snapshots—children, grandchildren, great-grandchildren, and spouses of those married—and arranged the pictures into family groups. With framed ornaments on a tree during the Christmas season, and a framed collage of every family member that hung in her home year round, Lillie kept her family close.

Rather than being in the forefront, Lillie chose to stay in the background. Rather than receiving, Lillie chose to give—to her husband and children, to extended family, and to her Lord whom she faithfully served for more than seventy years.

Each member of Lillie's family has a favorite story that shows her in a servant's role. Her grandchildren remember her for her banana pudding and cookies, and also for many less tangible, yet beautiful, expressions of her love. Lillie caught a squirrel and put it in a cage so granddaughter Marcy would have a playmate. She saved bread sacks and filled them with crusts and stale bread for Lori and other grandchildren, even grown-up grandchildren with a boyfriend, to feed to ducks at nearby Mobile Municipal Park.

As Lillie drew profiles of brides in wedding attire, granddaughter Debbi visualized herself in a white dress and dreamed of having a marriage just like her grandmother's lifelong love affair. Years later Debbi chose her grandmother, Lillie, to be the first person to see her engagement ring. Granddaughter Gaye recalls that while still in her nightclothes, Lillie served orange juice every year on Christmas morning to three sleepy granddaughters while they were still in bed. Lillie hid the dyed eggs on Easter Sunday afternoon. Young Sharla was delighted when she saw her basket filled with eggs that Lillie "found."

Daughter-in-law Donna misses buying and planting flowers for Lillie each spring. "She was always so appreciative . . . but I was the one who received the most 'joy' from her flower garden! Her joy and delight was a priceless gift to this South Carolina daughter-in-law."

Lillie lovingly attended to her husband's needs after he suffered a stroke and developed dementia and congestive heart failure. Even though her own health was failing, her concern was for her mate. In April 1999, skilled nursing care was required and Lenhardt was admitted to Cogburn Nursing Home. Little more than a month later Lillie was faced with an inoperable occurrence of earlier cancer.

Daughter-in-law Donna misses buying and planting flowers for Lillie each spring. "She was always so appreciative . . . but I was the one who received the most 'joy' from her flower garden! Her joy and delight was a priceless gift to this South Carolina daughter-in-law."

"When we left the doctor's office the day Mom got her report, we stopped at Morrison's Cafeteria," Melba says. "She had been having tests all morning and had not eaten. While in the cafeteria Mom said she needed to go to the restroom. I stood up to go with her, but she assured me that she was fine and would be right back. When she did not return I checked on her and found her crying. She had wanted to cry alone because she did not want to upset me. Mom had so much to deal with, yet her concern, as always, was for others. Mom returned to the table, finished eating, and told me she wanted to go to the nursing facility to see Dad.

"It was 'singing day' at the nursing home and a husband-wife team was singing old favorites, Gospel songs. With tears in her eyes Mom watched as Dad sang along with the couple. Every time he glanced her way she would smile as if to say, 'Everything is fine. I love you.' Her concern was for him and not for herself," Melba says.

Lillie was able to return once more to see Lenhardt. The cancer progressed rapidly making it difficult for her to breathe. She refused to use the wheelchair she needed and chose to walk into the room rather than worry her husband. "The three of us sang together for the last time," Melba says. "Dad on the bass, Mom the alto, and I, in broken voice, carried the melody."

Lillie's health failed quickly. She spent her last days in Mercy Medical Hospice Care surrounded by her family. Even then her prayers were most often intercessory prayers for others. The family came first.

Sensing the end was near, the family arranged to bring Lenhardt from the nursing home to Lillie's hospice facility miles away. In a wheelchair beside her bed, Lenhardt leaned forward and helped by his sons, bent down and kissed his bride good-bye. It was a tender moment as he whispered, "I love you."

Lillie looked into the face of her mate and said "I love you. I'll see you in heaven." Those were the only words she spoke that day.

Lillie's giving, her life of service—influenced by godly parents—and her early lifestyle came from a heart bowed at the feet of her Lord. Two days later she bowed in the presence of her Savior.

Lillie Phillips Roper
August 9, 1916-July 27, 1999

Lillie's Favorite Hymn

WHAT A FRIEND WE HAVE IN JESUS

John. M. Scriven

What a friend we have in Jesus,
All our sins and griefs to bear;
What a privilege to carry
Everything to God in prayer.

O what peace we often forfeit,
Oh, what needless pain we bear,
All because we do not carry
Everything to God in prayer.

Have we trials and temptations?
Is there trouble anywhere?
We should never be discouraged;
Take it to the Lord in prayer!

Can we find a friend so faithful,
Who will all our sorrows share?
Jesus knows our every weakness;
Take it to the Lord in prayer!

Are we weak and heavy laden,
Cumbered with a load of care?
Precious Savior, still our refuge,
Take it to the Lord in prayer!

Do thy friends despise, forsake thee?
Take it to the Lord in prayer!
In His arms He'll take and shield thee,
Thou wilt find a solace there.

Your Sweet Silence

Debbi Sims

I remember you best for your sweet silence, never boasting, never critical, loud, or pretentious. Instead you were warm and reassuring, regal and poised—yet simple.

I recall those sweet silent looks you gave PawPaw, and that twinkle in your eye that caused each of us to wonder about the mystery you two shared. How we long for the language of love you so clearly understood!

I can still see your sweet glance across a room alive with holiday festivity. With a quiet infectious glee you throw your head back and shyly touch your fingers to your mouth; your hand gently brushes your crossed knee as you relish the fun and love that fills the room—this is your family.

Your ever-present concern was for our well-being. You ensured our needs for food, shelter, warmth, and happiness with your first question, "Aren't you hungry?" and your last bidding, "I love you and you be careful, now."

And finally in those last days, amid pain, near the end, you acknowledged life as good as you looked into the eyes of your youngest great-grandchild and said, "My sweet baby Sarah." Your tenderness for even the smallest of God's creatures touches me even now.

In your silence we reach for reminders of you—wanting to hold on to you, to be like you. We remember, we weep, and we say, "Thank you, Mamaw, for the legacy of sweet silent service."

A Recipe From Lillie's Kitchen

TWO PECAN PIES

2 cups white corn syrup

2 cups brown sugar

1 teaspoon salt

1 cup melted butter

1 tablespoon vanilla extract

6 eggs

2 cups shelled pecans

3 heaping tablespoons all-purpose flour

*Mix syrup, sugar, salt, butter, vanilla, eggs, and flour.
Beat and pour into 2 unbaked pie shells. Sprinkle pecans over the
top and bake at 350 degrees for 45 minutes.*

Dorothy
A Portrait of Redemption

"For God so loved the world,
that he gave his only begotten Son,
that whosoever believeth in him should not perish,
but have everlasting life."

(John 3:16, KJV)

Rain pelts the windshield as the car wipers, though working furiously, provide only momentary views of U. S. Highway 43. Alternating between praying for our own safety, and the safety of our children who were meeting us at Dorothy's house, I mentally question the wisdom of this weekend driving trip. Yet, our mission, meeting our son and daughter-in-love, Karen, to interview her grandmother, dictates that we must continue to inch forward toward Tuscaloosa, Alabama.

My knowledge of Dorothy is limited to vignettes—a wedding,

funerals, and brief visits in her home. But a rainy afternoon spent in her home makes me feel as if I've always known her soft smile and her gentle voice. I understand more completely Karen's love for this one she calls "Grandma Dorothy." And I wish I had just one more of those sugar cookies from the cookie jar on her kitchen table.

Dorothy was born prior to the Great Depression to Jasper and Jeannie Dunn. Her parents were members of Orezonia Baptist Church near Tuscaloosa, Alabama. Dorothy recalls attending the church only infrequently, usually for homecoming or on Decoration Day. Her mother and father were Christians, and Dorothy's life has mirrored her mother's outstanding Christian virtue, kindness.

He father died from pneumonia. The young widow was left with four children, including six-year-old Dorothy. Later her mother married a widower, Dee Griffin, who brought his five children into the marriage. "We lived and worked as sharecroppers on farmland owned by the Searcy family," Dorothy says. Her stepfather and the children, both boys and girls, planted fields, pulled corn, and picked cotton. Though there was little time for church attendance as they worked together, they often sang the old Gospel songs "Amazing Grace," " Farther Along," and "The Great Speckled Bird."

The family raised cows, pigs, and chickens, and each spring they planted their own vegetable garden. Dorothy's mother was the homemaker, always busy, canning green beans and tomatoes, making cucumber pickles or jellies and preserves from figs, apples, grapes, and blueberries. She made the girls dresses from feed sacks. "Mama was my role model," Dorothy says. "She worked hard and she taught me about kindness, patience, and generosity."

But a rainy afternoon spent in her home makes me feel as if I've always known her soft smile and her gentle voice. I understand more completely Karen's love for this one she calls "Grandma Dorothy." And I wish I had just one more of those sugar cookies from the cookie jar on her kitchen table.

Kindness, I think, a virtue she learned from her mother that is woven like a thread of gold into the fabric of Dorothy's life.

At night, with light provided by the fireplace and kerosene

lamps, the family shelled corn, and occasionally played dominoes or card games. The radio was used little during the week with battery power being saved for Saturday night and The Grand Ole Opry.

The children walked together two miles to school, during winter months trudging slowly on frozen ground. Dorothy loved school. "Miss Ryan was one of my teachers," she recalls. "There were two or three grades in the classroom but she took up a lot of time with me and often called on me to recite. She took a special interest in me." Perhaps Miss Ryan's interest played a small part in a gift Dorothy was soon to receive.

Sixth-grade graduation was a big event in the 1930s. The girls wore white dresses and Dorothy became the recipient of a beautiful dress from the Searcy family, a dress their daughter had worn, a dress, perhaps, a teacher remembered as she thought about her special student, Dorothy. The organdy dress had hand-crocheted pink roses around the neck as well as the hem of the flowing three-tiered skirt. A pink satin ribbon was tied in a bow at her waist.

"I thought I was really dressed up," Dorothy says as she laughs.

And she was. This may have been one of the most beautiful dresses Dorothy wore as a child. Thoughts of that special night surely were tucked away in her memory, but otherwise life remained the same. She continued to attend school and to help with family chores. But one day as she drew water from a spring near her home, she met the man that she would marry.

"Virgil was working nearby, logging in the woods, and he came to the spring to drink. He was a widower with children," Dorothy says. "Even though he was much older, I knew this was the man for me. I saw him often at a friend's house, and we wrote to each other. I met his children."

Peggy, the youngest child, remembers a Sunday afternoon when she was lying across the bed with her father. "Are you going

Sixth-grade graduation was a big event in the 1930s. The girls wore white dresses and Dorothy became the recipient of a beautiful dress from the Searcy family, a dress their daughter had worn, a dress, perhaps, a teacher remembered as she thought about her special student, Dorothy.

to marry Dorothy Jane?" the child asked.

"I don't know," her father replied.

To Peggy's delight, within months, Dorothy Dunn added Wakefield to her name on June 23, 1945. She became wife to Virgil and mother to his six children. The youngest, Peggy, was only three years old.

Peggy began to call Dorothy "Mama." Dorothy gently told the child, "I don't want to take the place of your mother. She should always have a special place in your heart. Just call me Dot." Yet she loved and cared for the children as if they were her own. Dorothy stepped into marriage both as wife to Virgil and as "Dot," a loving surrogate mother. A bond of love remains today between Dorothy and those children.

Virgil and his new wife moved the family to Mobile during World War II, then on to Georgia and back to Mobile before retiring in Tuscaloosa. Several children married and settled in the Mobile area so the couple returned frequently to visit children and grandchildren. It was during one of those trips that we witness God's redemptive plan unfolding in their lives.

"Virgil became ill one evening and was taken to the hospital emergency room," Dorothy says. "The doctors said he needed surgery immediately. When they operated they found he had colon cancer. I realized it was the end for him. We had heard the Gospel through music. But it was during Virgil's illness that the words, the messages of those hymns, really spoke to me, because I knew it was the end for him."

His granddaughter, Karen, tells the story. "Our family pastor, Rev. Mack Morris, visited Granddaddy in the intensive care unit after the surgery. One night Brother Mack woke up in the middle of the night and felt compelled to return to the hospital. In the hospital intensive care unit he presented the plan of salvation to Granddaddy, and he accepted Christ as his Savior. Granddaddy died just a few days later and was buried at Mount Olive Baptist Church in Tuscaloosa."

Dorothy lost her mate. In losing her mate she, too, found a Savior.

"After my husband's death I attended Mount Olive Church every Sunday. From July to January I was in church. I heard the salvation story many times," Dorothy says. "I was in church but that was all. I had not made a decision, but I knew that I needed to accept Christ."

In a letter dated "Monday night, 11:30 P.M., January 14, 1974," Dorothy wrote to her granddaughter Karen about her conversion experience:

> Hi Karen,
>
> … I was saved this morning. I've cried all day, but tears of joy. I wanted to call but I knew all I would do was cry.
>
> Karen, I don't have to tell you the feeling I have. You already know. I have been under conviction since the day of the funeral. It was all I could do to hold back when Bro. Mack gave the altar call.
>
> I have been so upset, running, trying to escape. And yet the words (at the funeral) were meant for me. Brother Wayne came over to see me last week but after I had gone to work. This morning I heard this knock, and I came up front and I saw him at the door.
>
> We talked social for awhile. Then he began to ask questions like, what church I belonged to. I told him I didn't. I was just a big lost sinner. And it all started from there. And when it

was all over I was a newborn child.

He told me whatever church I wanted to join was my decision. If it was Mount Olive, he would be more than happy to have me and if I wanted to be baptized at that time, to bring my clothes. I told him that's where I wanted to be.

I won't say he was as happy as I (was), but he was happy. Thanks to all for your prayers. I have felt them each time. And tell Bro. Mack and Kathy I appreciate their prayers and kind words. They have also been a part of this new life. And I'll still need the prayers of all of you.

Love to all,

Dot

The next Sunday morning, January 20, 1974, Dorothy made a public profession of faith at Mount Olive Baptist Church in Tuscaloosa and, in another white dress made for this special occasion, was baptized by Rev. Wayne Styres.

Rev. Styres moved to other pastorates but has retired and returned to Tuscaloosa. I talked with him by telephone. "Yes, I do remember Dorothy. I know her well," he said. "I visited with her and asked about her relationship to Christ. I shared the Gospel with her and she prayed to receive Christ. I baptized her. She was a quiet lady but faithful. She volunteered to work the afternoon shift at Partlow Hospital so she could attend Sunday School and the morning worship service—a faithful and beautiful Christian lady."

A beautiful Christian lady, I think, a portrait of God's redeeming grace provided by the death of Christ and offered freely to all that ask for forgiveness of sin.

Though almost thirty years have passed, the events of that day are etched in Dorothy's mind. Smiling and speaking softly, Dorothy describes the excitement of that day. She called family and friends and shared with them her early morning experience and the joy she felt. And she wrote her letters. Karen's letter was just one of many she wrote late that night as she shared with distant family her salvation experience.

I ask if she had ever had doubts about what happened that morning.

"Never!" she exclaims. "I have never doubted!"

"It was raining the morning that Rev. Styres came," Dorothy says. But when he left, it was a beautiful day—still raining outside, but a beautiful day for me. I wanted to tell everyone what had happened!"

Listening to her joy, and the story she shared so freely that day, I am reminded of the words of the great hymn written by Fanny Crosby.

"Redeemed! how I love to proclaim it!
Redeemed by the blood of the Lamb;
Redeemed through His infinite mercy,
His child, and forever, I am."

Dorothy's Favorite Hymn

SINCE JESUS CAME INTO MY HEART

Rufus McDaniel

What a wonderful change in my life has been wrought
Since Jesus came into my heart!
I have light in my soul for which long I have sought,
Since Jesus came into my heart!

I have ceased from my wandering and going astray,
Since Jesus came into my heart!
And my sins which were many are all washed away,
Since Jesus came into my heart!

I'm possessed of a hope that is steadfast and sure,
Since Jesus came into my heart!
Now no dark clouds of doubt now my pathway obscure,
Since Jesus came into my heart!

I shall go there to dwell in that city, I know,
Since Jesus came into my heart!
And I'm happy, so happy, as onward I go,
Since Jesus came into my heart!

Chorus:

Since Jesus came into my heart!

Since Jesus came into my heart!

Floods of joy o'er my soul like the sea billows roll,

Since Jesus came into my heart.

Dorothy's Favorite Recipe

MY BUTTER COOKIES

3 sticks butter (not margarine)

1 cup sugar

1 egg, unbeaten

1 teaspoon vanilla

4 cups flour

Cream butter and sugar; add eggs and vanilla.

Add the flour gradually.

Roll into sticks on waxed paper and chill (or freeze).

Cut thin and bake 10 minutes at 350 degrees until golden brown.

NOTE FROM DOROTHY: Store frozen rolls in freezer.

When you need a quick treat, bake and share.

NOTE FROM THE AUTHOR: Delicious!

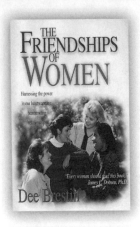
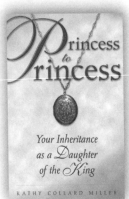